ALMOST FREE

MONEY

How to Make Significant Money from Free Materials You Can
Find Anywhere, Including Garage Sales, Scrap Metal, and
Discarded Items

By Eric Michael

Table of Contents

INTRODUCTION

Welcome to the fun and exciting world of Almost Free Money. I know what you are thinking. There must be some sort of catch, right? If there was money to be made for free, than everybody would be doing it. It can't be that easy.

I'm here to tell you that I have been finding free items and materials and selling them online for over twelve years. I have sold over 10,000 items on the internet, and almost all of them cost me under $1. I sell over 90% of these items for over $5, and I have sold a ton of items for over $25, and I currently have an inventory on Amazon worth well over $30,000. I am not bragging, I am presenting these facts as inspiration. If I can build this type of business while still working a demanding full-time job in a rural area, so can you.

The great thing about this business is its flexibility. You can find inventory and free stuff at any time and in any location around the world. You can put as much effort and time into this "job" as you want to. Obviously, the harder you work, the more money you will make, but if you are tied up with work or your family, you can make good money with very little time spent. If you are temporarily unemployed, a stay-at-home parent, or on disability, you can find inventory from home. As a matter of fact, this book starts right off by giving you step-by-step directions on how to find items and materials that are already at your home or property that you can quickly turn into "free money"!

If you have never sold anything on eBay or Amazon, I will get you up and running, so that you are selling on both websites. If you only sell exclusively on either website, I will tell you why you should diversify, and the advantages and disadvantage of selling on each respective site.

If you are an internet re-selling veteran, which I am predicting that many of the readers of this book will be, I will provide you information that I could not find anywhere else, and I have done a lot of internet research and read quite a variety of books and Kindle e-books.

My specialty in the last twelve years has been finding items that are completely free, or that cost me under twenty-five cents. I will show you what my hundreds of hours of research yielded over the last twelve years. As a matter of fact, at the end of this document there is a list of over 500 items and materials that I have located for under $1, and then re-sold for excellent profits. I will show you how to do your own online research, so that you can find similar results, and expand your knowledge base.

I am also going to broaden your horizons by adding selling scrap into your repertoire. Selling scrap metal is beneficial to internet sellers for several reasons. Number one, scrap metal is always available. You can find it anywhere. You can save your family hundreds of dollars a year just by saving items that you are may be throwing in your trash. Selling scrap metal also allows sellers to minimize the loss of unsold eBay and Amazon items. I will show you how to make very good money by parting out vintage electronics that you can find for free and then sell the resulting components online and other portions at a scrap metal dealer for maximum value.

We will discuss many different items and materials to sell, the easiest and most profitable places to sell your finds, and some tips for enhancing your profits and creating your own niche so that you can sell items that make you money and are enjoyable for you to locate.

I will explore several different venues for locations that you can find inventory. Chances are, if you are reading this book, you probably enjoy finding bargains at garage sales, yard sales, and second-hand stores such as Goodwill. I will show you how to take the next step and re-sell your bargains for maximum profit. I will explain how to organize your inventory hunting, how to find items for free at garage sales that you can re-sell, how to get the most inventory items from each sale, and how to figure out which sales have the potential for the best items by reading classified advertisements.

I will take the reader on a trip to a scrap metal dealer, where I describe in detail how easy it is to sell scrap metal for the first time by yourself, and with no training required.

Perhaps most importantly, the reader will learn where to go to conduct their own research and find even more sources of income. Being able to effectively research income sources is the most important aspect of a growing small business. I will provide the reader with a number of links to internet sites with invaluable information on a variety of topics that you can use to make money.

Many of these internet sites were created by businesspersons with decades of knowledge on their particular subjects, and many have made at least six figure incomes in their niches. These sites have outstanding explanations on locating and selling free (or almost free) materials for profit, and most of the sites provide detailed images of what to look for.

If you are a visually-oriented learner, you will be using the hyperlinks that I provide in this document frequently to refer to these internet sites that have photographic images and diagrams, in order to visualize the meaning of my text descriptions.

Also provided to complement this document are appendices that contain over four hundred individual items and materials that you can find anywhere for free (or almost free), and details where to sell them for profit. These lists are broken down into categories: Usable Items, EBay Collectibles, Organic Items, and Items with Defined Values.

To use the EBay category numbers provided within the appendix lists, simply type or cut-and-paste the number into the category box when making your auction on the EBay or Auctiva (an auction listing website discussed later in the document) listing page.

I also provide you with over twenty excellent sources to advance your knowledge base with further reading on the internet. Most of these websites are specific areas that you can explore to add even more selling platforms onto your existing portfolios. Many of these sources have provided their authors with stand-alone five and six figure incomes.

START-UP: INITIAL ASSESSMENT

Before we get into the nuts and bolts of this document, it's important for you to understand several things about yourself. First, what do you hope to accomplish by using this information? Are you looking for a second income? Are you time-strapped, and only have time to save your family a little money? Are you considering a new business opportunity?

In my opinion, you should always leave yourself the opportunity to expand your efforts into at least a significant second income. What the heck, it costs you very little money to obtain your selling inventory, and there is the potential to make fairly easy profits. Why not take advantage of that?

I started out buying collectible items at garage sales for 5-25 cents, and then re-selling them on EBay for up to $250 an item. That was a cash cow for a while, but as more and more people found out how easy it was to sell on EBay, the competition got fierce, and the amount of collectibles in the marketplace drove the selling prices way down. So, I started researching other ways to diversify, so I did not have to rely so much on collectible items.

Now, I prefer selling items that people are always going to need, and also have a value that is determined outside of popular demand. I enjoy finding items for free while I am recreating, and then sell them for easy cash. I mean really, if you're going to have a serious hobby, make it one that actually makes you money. Why throw away big money on a golf course, when you can spend your time shopping for investment items at yard sales?

As I started adding new avenues for income, I found that I could use my "hobby" as a second income for my family, and my wife could stay home with our young children, instead of her working and then having to pay for childcare. Obviously, that was a huge incentive to step it up and go for it.

When we started making significant money, I knew that we needed a business plan. There are thousands of people selling odds and ends on EBay and other places online. The ones that actually make significant money are the people who: #1: ARE NOT LAZY, #2: Have common sense, and #3: Are resourceful and are willing to do some research.

I started thinking of my second income as a business. I claimed my earnings on my income taxes, so that I could write off business expenses, such as vehicle mileage and meals while I was finding inventory or going to the scrap metal dealer. I kept track of receipts. I knew how much actual profit I was making after subtracting gas cost and EBay listing fees. I wrote off a home office and storage room deductions on my income taxes. All of these things are actually very easy to do, and make you more money for your business.

Even if you are thinking that you are only going to sell some items and materials from around your home, I can guarantee you that if you put some effort into it, you will at least expand into having your family, friends and neighbors save you items that they would normally throw away, and then you, too, will be on your way to an easy second income. So, what I am saying to you is this - you might as well save yourself even more money, and start right out thinking of this as a business.

What does thinking of your re-selling as a business mean? You have to consider more than just your initial cost and end sales price for an item and/or material that you have sold. The biggest mistake beginners make is not considering the actual cost of selling a particular item.

For instance, consider two potential sales items. The first is a book that you find at a garage sale for 25 cents and then re-sell for $20 on EBay. The second is a box of insulated electrical cords that you have collected at your house and then sell at the scrap metal dealer for $20. Which is actually the better sale?

The answer is: It depends! All things being equal, the box of cords ends up being the better deal, because the only time that you had into prepping the cords was about five seconds to cut the plugs off and stuff the cords into a box. In order to sell the book on EBay, you have to: 1) photograph the book 2) upload the photos 3) type up the listing, and 4) package the item for shipping. Time is money, and you have to take that into account.

However, if you live in a rural area, and the nearest scrap metal dealer is 45 minutes away from your house, you have the additional travel time and gas money to account for. You have to remember that some avenues may seem on the surface to be great deals, but by the time you factor in your time in preparation, hard work and gas money, they may not be your best alternative in making money. You are looking for things that you enjoy doing anyway, have a renewable supply of, and are comfortable in selling. You also want to be able to sell the items quickly and without an overabundance of preparation time.

The last thing that you have to consider before starting is, how much storage room do you have available to you? There are a lot of items that you can make good profits on that take up a lot of room. Do you have room to disassemble vehicles or appliances on your property? Do you have room in your home for large bookshelves for storing books or music inventory?

If not, you will have to concentrate on smaller items to sell, or items that you know that you can sell almost immediately. Your significant other is not going to want to have your stuff lying all over his or her counters, or in boxes on the floors in your home.

HOW AND WHERE TO SELL

Before you start accumulating items and materials to sell, it is important to have a good idea where you are going to sell it. Finding the good stuff to sell is only half of the battle. You need to know where to go to get top dollar when you go to re-sell it.

In my experience, the best and quickest way to sell many things is to sell them on EBay. While the sales prices on many items have come down over the last five years or so, there is always going to be a market on EBay for items that people need, and you can't beat the convenience and potential deals on EBay for the bargain hunter.

Even if you are intimidated by selling on the internet or don't have the desire to do so, you should still be familiar with how EBay works and how to sell an item there. It will not take you long at all in this line of business to figure out that EBay is the best location to sell many different types of materials, including some that you may have previously thought were only sold elsewhere. Scrap metal is one example.

Consider this. If you sell copper to your local scrap metal dealer, you are selling to a middle-man. Your dealer still has to sell your copper again to a metal wholesaler for his business to make any money, so you are therefore offered considerably less for your scrap on the deal, right?

On EBay, you offer the same box of scrap copper to thousands of scrap dealers and investors. The bidding on your lot is determined by the free market and the spot copper price, not by an individual scrap metal dealer, who often has very little competition in his local marketplace.

Just about anything you can think of that is bought and sold in any physical marketplace is also sold on EBay. We will get further in depth into the world of EBay in later chapters, but just realize for now that EBay gives you the best opportunity to diversify your sales, and the potential for buyers to bid higher on items than you may have thought the item was worth to begin with.

I remember in our first year of internet selling, my wife and I were shopping at a garage sale. We had a few odds and ends that we were going to buy, and my wife saw a cheap looking plastic beer sign in the ten-cent box near the pay table. She picked it out on a whim, and we paid for our stuff and left. The sign was only about 4 x 8" in size, and made of a thin Plexiglas material.

We offered the sign at auction on EBay, starting at 99 cents, and a week later, two competing bidders had raised the ending price to almost $250! The winner e-mailed us and asked if we had any more signs from the beer company that was advertising with the sign my wife had found. He informed us that the beer company was a popular brand in the state that he was from, and that the brewery had gone out of business over twenty years ago. The signs were impossible to find and were very collectible. Who knew?!

SELLING ON EBAY AND AMAZON

I am not going to devote a lot of time in this document to the subject of beginning to sell items online, only because the websites have done such an excellent job of making it easy for anybody to understand the process of listing items.

Both EBay and Amazon have intentionally designed their listing pages so that you can list items regardless of your internet skills and writing abilities. You will typically only have to type a paragraph or two at the most to describe your items, and simple descriptions often are better than profuse flourishing praise for your items, so do not feel bad if you are not a wordsmith.

Both websites also provide tutorials and FAQ's (Frequently Asked Questions) that are linked to the beginning listing pages. These documents are designed so that even if it you have never turned on a computer, you can still figure out how to get an item listed on their sites. Then, once you have listed your first item, it is very easy to list in subsequent sessions. Once you are signed in, EBay provides you with a link from the initial listing page that allows you to bring up several of the last auctions that you designed to use as a template for listing new auctions.

First, we will discuss how to begin selling on EBay. The only equipment that you will need is: A computer with internet access (high speed internet is a huge advantage, but not required), a digital camera, and a scale for weighing items.

We are going to go step-by-step, and list a collectible book that we will pretend that you found in a free box at a garage sale.

First, look at your book. Can you improve its desirability in an auction setting? People bid on items in EBay listings based on two things; the image(s) of the item and your item description.   So, if you can make the digital pictures that you take look better by cleaning up your item a bit before taking the photos, by all means, do so. If the book has a vinyl dust jacket, carefully wipe the outer surface to remove any dust and dirt build-up. If there are price stickers that can be peeled off without damaging the surface of the cover, remove them.

You are now able to use multiple pictures for free on EBay, so take several pictures of your book, including several photos of the cover, any nice interior illustrations, interesting text, and any condition issues that the bidder will want to see. The more pictures that you provide, the better off you are going to be, and the higher the ending price will be on your auctions. Remember, that almost every consumer buys items based primarily on the visual appearance of what they are buying, so give bidders what they are looking for!

Upload the digital photos to your computer. If you have never uploaded photos, EBay provides directions on the process. When you upload, start a folder for the items you are going to be selling in your 'My Pictures' Folder on your computer, or put it on your desktop, so that you can find the folder easily when you go to download photos to auctions or listing pages.

Go to your computer and log on to the internet, and go to the EBay site.   At the top of the page, there is a link for 'Sell'. Click on the link. If you have never sold on EBay, you will need to register, and provide personal and financial information so that you can get paid for your sales through PayPal. PayPal is EBay's payment collection site.   After you have registered or signed in, go the listing page. You may elect to complete the tutorial the first time you sell. It walks you through each segment of the listing page. It is very user-friendly and allows you to quickly move through the listing page.

Make sure that you weigh your item accurately, so that you can provide the weight of the item for shipping purposes. Don't try to estimate the weight, or you will end up either paying for part of the shipping out of your own pocket, or charging winning bidders too much for shipping and consequently making your customers angry. You may also elect to allow 'Free U.S. shipping' for your item, which alleviates all of these issues altogether. Just make sure that you pick a starting price that is high enough so that you can make a minimum profit on the item after you add in the shipping costs that you are going to have to pay for.

Everything else in the listing page is self-explanatory. There are also links next to each heading on the listing page, in case you do not understand something.

Two of the most important things to consider when building an auction are the item's title and the cover photograph. These are what potential bidders use to determine whether they are going to click on your auction and then hopefully bid on your item. Ensure that your image is clear and that you can tell what the item is. Remember, the image thumbnail boxes are fairly small on the EBay auctions pages. Also, anything that makes your image stand out is helpful. Make your photo as colorful or distinct as possible. If your item is not very exciting, you may decide to give your item a colorful or textured backdrop by setting your item on colorful material for the photo, or taking your photo while your item is against a brightly painted wall.

The item's title should also accurately and completely describe it, without making it sound "over-the-top". Make sure that you include brand names and dates the item what manufactured, if you know them. With books, make sure that you have the title, author, and edition number.

In the item description, describe the condition of the item as accurately as possible. Do not try to make your item sound better than it is so that you can make a couple of extra dollars on it.   Also, list any other description detractions that are not visible in the photographs that you provided.

List your item. When the auction ends in seven days (unless you specified fewer days), EBay notifies the winning bidder by e-mail that they have won your auction. Payment is made through PayPal, and then you are notified, along with the winner's shipping information.   Securely package the item, and ship to the address provided. It is as easy as that.

Another very easy website to sell on is Amazon. If the item that you want to sell is a media item or has a bar code, it is probably available to sell on Amazon. Selling on Amazon is extremely fast and easy. It is also profitable.

All you have to do to sell on Amazon is open a selling account. You will have to provide a checking or savings account for Amazon to deposit your money into, but it is a huge secure marketplace with thousands of sellers. Don't worry about providing your financial information.

Before signing up, determine how many items you will be selling on the site. When you get to the point that you will be consistently selling at least 40 individual items a month on Amazon, you should upgrade to a premium sellers account. The upgraded account eliminates a $1 fee that is charged on each item sold for sellers with a normal seller account. It also allows you to sell some items that normal sellers cannot, and you can also make your own item pages, which I use regularly for selling rare collectible items. The price for the premium account is currently $39.95.

To list your items on Amazon, all you have to do is locate the item within the marketplace by doing a search for that item. For instance, if you wanted to sell a copy of the Nirvana 'Nevermind' CD, you would search for it in the 'Music' category.   You can either type in 'Nirvana Nevermind' into the search bar at the top of the page, or if you have the CD in hand, you can type in the bar code number on the back of the CD. It is always found below the bar code, and includes the smaller numbers at the beginning and end of the bar code. For U.S. items, the bar code has 10 numbers, and for European items, sometimes there are 13 numbers. For books and media items, there is usually an ISBN number provided on the title page or on the item cover that you can type in.

When you find the correct item page, there is a link that says 'Sell Your Item' on the right side of the page. You click on that button, and then simply type in your description of the condition of the item, enter your asking price, and then click 'complete', and your item is for sale on Amazon. It is very quick and easy.

When a potential buyer goes to the Nirvana 'Nevermind' page to buy the CD, they see a number of individual listings for that CD, along with your listing. The buyer chooses the copy that they want to buy, based on the price and condition description provided. The buyer clicks 'buy' to complete the sale. There is no bidding, as on EBay. You do not have to take photographs for your item, or making time consuming listings. If the buyer picks your item, Amazon takes a closing fee from your selling price, gives you a shipping credit and then deposits the balance into your account.

When you get enough money in your Amazon balance, you can then deposit it directly into your personal bank account, or Amazon does it automatically for you every two weeks.

You can see that there are advantages to selling on Amazon versus EBay. First, it is much easier and faster to list items. I can list a box full of CDs in about a half an hour on Amazon. It's also free to list items. You don't get charged until someone buys your item through the Amazon marketplace. You can build an inventory without any upfront cost. On eBay, you are charged a listing fee for each individual auction listed, whether the item sells at auction, or ends without a bid.

Amazon can also be a catch-22 proposition for selling items, in that you may sell your item the same day you list it for more than you can sell it for at auction on EBay. However, you could also list a great $100 collectible book on Amazon, and it may sit there on your shelf for over a year before the right buyer comes along and buys it from you, or it may never sell at all.

You are also constantly competing with other sellers' prices listed on Amazon. You could have the only copy of a collectible item available on the Amazon marketplace for months for $250, and then have another Amazon seller list the same item for significantly less than your price, and then steal your sale when it is purchased several days later from that other seller.

Amazon also charges what I would consider exorbitant selling fees when your item sells; significantly higher than EBay's closing and listing fees combined. Amazon knows that they have very little competition in their niche, and they take advantage of that.

The seller has a number of things to weigh when determining where to sell online. How quickly do you want your money? Do you have room to store items for a period of time? Is it more important for you to maximize profit per item, or sell items fast for a bit less money? Is your item collectible and therefore may do better on EBay, where bidders can see photos of your cool looking item, and also let you tell them about the item in your description? There are also other places to sell online, and after you determine your own niche, you may decide to build a website, but to begin with, EBay and Amazon are the two easiest online sites to begin selling on.

There are also many physical stores that you can sell items to. Collectible items can be sold to stores that specialize in selling collectibles, such as Sports Collectibles shops. They can also be sold to pawn shops, antique stores, etc. The most important thing about selling your item to these people is YOU HAVE TO KNOW HOW MUCH YOUR ITEM IS WORTH BEFORE you go the store to sell it. Period. Do your research online and find current values for commodities with spot prices, like gold and silver items, or search completed listings on EBay for similar items. Do NOT allow a pawn shop owner to swindle you.

You have to realize that while you will get cash in hand at these types of places, you will not get full value for your items. The shop owner has to make a profit when he or she sells your item again. You will almost always get more for your item online than at a physical store. You have to weigh ease of selling and immediate sales against maximum profit and more prep time selling online.

WHERE TO FIND ITEMS TO SELL

It's surprisingly easy to find cheap stuff to sell. It's all around you, and you probably don't even know it. Let's start with your home. Hopefully, somebody at your house is a pack-rat and you haven't had a garage sale in several years. Here's the most important thing to remember. Almost everything has a value to somebody. You just have to find that person or group of people to sell your stuff to.

Start looking around your house, and then look again. The second time, try to see your belongings through a collector's eyes. Do you have any old toys that are collectible? How about your old biker's jackets, vintage T-shirts or retro dresses? All of this stuff is collectible. Do you have old books or comics? What about your old collection of marbles, baseball cards, or buttons? These are all collectible. What about that old box of stuff your uncle gave you with his old racing trophies and the broken Commodore 64 computer in it? Yep. Collectible.

Once you start looking, you will be surprised what people collect. Old playing cards, yes. Matchbooks, yes. Beer caps and cans. Yes. Just start gathering stuff that you look at and say, hmm… maybe somebody collects this. If somebody ever thought that the item was cool, I will guarantee you that somebody still thinks it's cool today, and therefore worth money. I'll show you how to determine value later.

Another place you can make some quick money is with non-functional electronics and appliances. If it's been broken for a long time, it may very well be collectible and worth fixing now.

Several years ago, I found a Simon electronic game in a 'Free' box in a garage sale. I grabbed it and brought it home. It didn't work, so I opened the battery compartment. It only needed the terminals cleaned, and it worked like new. I sold it in a week for $50. It is amazing how often broken stuff can be fixed for free and with very little effort.

Also, high-end equipment can be sold for parts, even if it is not repairable. For instance, the cushioned feet on high-end audio equipment can sell for $25, and that's just for the feet. Many of the components can be sold on EBay, even if the item hasn't worked in years!

You can also scrap larger appliances for scrap value. Junk computers may have $20 or more in scrap gold, silver, and copper inside them, as well as having usable components that you can sell separately. The trick is to find where on EBay to sell the scrap and parts.

If you are willing to do some work, you can even scrap whole vehicles and sell many of the resulting parts on EBay. Then, you can scrap the remaining steel auto body for up to $250 at a scrap yard.

Do you have any decaying cars, snowmobiles, or lawnmowers in your yard or pole barn? Have any 25 year old bikes in your garage? They are probably worth at least $50 apiece. You can see where I'm going here. Check the list at the end of the book for more ideas about things to look for.

The bottom line is, if you have something that you can sell at a garage sale, you can probably sell it for considerably more on EBay.

Now that you have cleared out your collectibles, move on to clothing. Vintage clothing should be sold individually. Many jackets, headwear, suits, ties, shoes, dresses, etc. can sell for more than what you would think on EBay. Next, gather your clothing that is in good shape, but you don't wear anymore, or the kids have outgrown. You can sell clothes lots on EBay for good profit, or you can take them to a second-hand store and set up an account and have them sell clothes for you there. You get a percentage of each sale. Take your remaining clothes and put them in your Goodwill box. Keep track of what's in the box, because you will be writing the value off on your income taxes.

Next, if you have kids, gather all of their toys and games that they have outgrown or don't play with. Check Amazon first. I was amazed by what I have been able sell used toys for on Amazon. It the toy has a box with a bar code, it's very easy to find and sell them. Type in the numbers under the bar code into the Amazon search bar.

Even toys without boxes can be sold by searching for the name of the toy. This is true even of smaller Tonka toys, action figures, baby toys, etc. Although they may sometimes take a while to sell, they often sell for a lot more than on EBay. Board games can sell very well on Amazon, too, but toys can sometimes take a long time to get off your shelves.

What you don't list on Amazon, check on EBay. If your toy or groups of toys have sold well on EBay in completed listings, make a listing and sell them. Remember to always check discarded toys for usable batteries before listing them or getting rid of them. Batteries are expensive! They also add to the shipping weight, and should not be shipped inside of toys or electronics for fear of the batteries leaking and causing damage.

OK. All of the toys that have not been listed on Amazon and EBay can be put in a box. Cut off anything with a copper wire or brass pieces and save them. Look and see if there is anything worth disassembling for parts. Tip: I have sold battery compartment covers, cases for electronic games, board game pieces, and lots of other parts that are easily broken or lost on EBay for good money.

Everything that can't be sold or scrapped should go in the Goodwill box. Write down all of the toys in the box for your taxes.

Next go to your storage areas, closets and attic. Go through all of your junk boxes. Take out everything that might be collectible and check values in EBay completed listings. Most any everyday item that is usable and in good condition can also be sold on EBay. Put all of your electronics and appliances in one area. If they work, check completed listings and see if they have value on EBay. If they do have value, sell them. If they don't, scrap them for metal value. Keep metals separated, especially copper and brass. Many scrap dealers will also buy electronics by the pound for scrap value. You can sell the electric motors inside of electronics, as well as any parts containing solid copper (not wires) as 'copper breakage' for good money. I will provide you with a sample list from a scrap dealer that shows how to scrap appliances and what you can get per pound for the pieces.

Check all of your home décor items (knick-knacks, curios) on EBay to see if they are worth selling there. Many have decent value. Some you can group together in a lot (Hallmark ornaments, collectible plates, bells, etc.). If you have anything that looks like it is made of brass or is copper colored, check them with a magnet. If they don't stick to a magnet, they are pure copper or brass and should be sold as such. Currently, spot price for copper is over $3 a pound and brass is over $2 a pound. You can either save these metals for scrap value, or sell on EBay if you think you can make more than the spot price per pound. If you have high value items like Longaberger baskets, nice antiques, or Hummel figurines, make sure you know what they are worth before listing them, or have them appraised. They can be worth big bucks.

Now go to the garage or tool shed. Take any power tool that you don't use and see if it still works. If it does, and there is value on EBay, sell it there. Most power tools sell well on EBay. If it does not have value and the tool has a rechargeable battery, the batteries are often worth as much as the whole tool, if the battery has good life left. The battery charger should also be sold with the battery, or separately if the battery is bad. Hand tools can be sold in lots or individually, in some cases. Everything left that is metal, put in your scrap metal pile. Anything electric that doesn't work should at least have the power cord cut off for copper scrap. Heavier items should be disassembled for copper breakage and other scrap value. Check anything that contains a battery to see if the batteries or battery holders are usable or sellable.

We have completed the home sweep. You probably found a bunch of other sellable stuff that I didn't mention once you got going. You now also know where to look for good stuff in your relatives and friends homes. Most of the time they'll give you this stuff for free, especially if you are willing to do some work and clean up the boxes and other stuff lying around their homes for them. Additionally, metals like copper, non-magnetic aluminum and brass can be easily collected in a small box by your family and friends, and then you can pick up the boxes periodically when you visit them. Perhaps you feel generous, and decide to give them a little cash for their trouble.

Once you have practiced at home, you will come up with all sorts of places to find similar items for cheap. Sellers at garage sales, second-hand stores, Salvation Armies, Goodwill Stores and flea markets often have not done their homework on what they have for sale, and you can get high-end items for often under a dollar, especially at garage sales. Check road-sides for free metal, especially anything with a power cord.

FINDING INVENTORY ONLINE

There are also numerous places to find items to sell online. Finding items from your computer or portable device can be particularly advantageous if you are tied to a desk at work or only have time to look for inventory when most physical stores are closed.

Bargains abound on EBay and Craig's List, but you have to consider that you are competing with other resellers for your items to sell, and it will cost you more to get your source material to sell than it would if you found the same item at a garage sale. You also have to consider that on top of the higher cost per item, you will also probably have to pay shipping costs for your items.

Despite the issues I have mentioned, there are definitely profits to be made on many items listed on EBay. So… What are we looking for exactly, you ask? The trick is to be smarter and/or more diligent than your competing sellers on EBay. You want to win your items for the lowest possible ending price (net ending price, including shipping costs).

I have had very good luck winning large lots of items, such as boxes of books, and then re-listing individual books from the lots on EBay or Amazon. I have found several $100 books and quite a few $50 collectible books in bulk lots of books that I won for under $5. I have also won a number of books and other collectibles for 99 cents, which I immediately re-listed with a better listing page and resold for over $50.

Here are some quick pointers. Do not bid until the last minute of an online auction if at all possible. Many auctions do not get bids at all, especially obscure collectibles that are valuable only to a select few. These items can be very profitable, if you have the ability to find people that collect them. You may have to re-list these items multiple times, or allow them to sit in your Amazon inventory for months. But, they have the potential to make big profits.

Items that do have bids tend to draw the competition's attention, and if you bid early, someone will often outbid you at the last second. There are 'auction sniping' programs and applications that can help you win bids at the very last second, but they cost money. It's up to you to determine if you think the program is worth the added expense.

Look for inventory when you don't have a lot of competing bidders. You can steal auctions late at night, on holidays, and early in the morning.

You are also looking for the lazy sellers' auction items or lots. Try to find the lots in which the seller did not do his or her homework and does not know the value of the items. Look for misspelled words and author's or musician's names. Look for short descriptions that don't specify content. For instance, an EBay listing titled only 'Grammas old books' would definitely catch my attention for several reasons. Number one, the books are probably going to be older and potentially collectible. Number two, the seller is lazy and not very bright. They cannot spell 'grandma', and they didn't care enough to tell the bidders what kind of books are in the lot and whether they were valuable.

I typically search specific category locations where bulk lots are listed like music, books, or collectibles. You are given check boxes on the top of the page that allows you to sort by 'best match', 'lowest price', etc. I click on 'lowest price, plus shipping', which gives you the entire category listed, with the lowest priced items, plus shipping costs added in at the top.

Usually you have to sift through a bunch of garbage for the first couple of pages, but sometimes you will find a gem. You can also sort by auctions 'Ending Soonest' to see the auctions that are very close to ending. That can also help you win excellent lots or items.

When I find interesting auctions to bid on, I 'Watch' the auctions. Watching auctions allows you to easily come back to the auction at a later date or time if the price at the end of the auction is still to your liking. Simply go to your 'My EBay' page, click on your 'Bidding' link and check the auctions that you are watching. If you are watching a number of items, you should leave yourself a note somewhere where you will see it often, reminding you of what the item is, when it ends, and how high you are willing to bid to win the auction. It's easy to get tied up with something else and miss the end of an auction that you really wanted to win without placing a bid.

Another idea is to search for a specific title, instead of looking in your usual categories. A lot of times, sellers will accidentally list items in the wrong category by forgetting to change the category when they are listing many auctions at once (Yes, I've done it, too.). Some sellers just do not know where to sell items, and list them in the wrong locations, as well.

There are additional considerations with EBay auctions. Don't get burned by a lazy or dishonest seller. EBay provides bidders with information to avoid some of these problems. After a person wins an auction and receives the item that they won, they are given an opportunity to provide 'feedback' to other potential bidders, regarding their buying experience for that particular seller. Each seller is given a feedback score that tells you how many feedbacks they have received. It also has a positive feedback percentage to the right of the seller's name. If the seller has had over 100 feedbacks, and a score of over 95%, they are probably a reliable seller. You can also read individual feedbacks by clicking on the feedback number, and you can read what other buyers had to say about their experience with that seller.

You also want to CAREFULLY read the descriptions of the items that you are potentially bidding on, and make sure that you understand what the seller is listing. It seems like that would be obvious, but quite often, sellers don't take the time to adequately describe items. Sometimes, they just don't have time because they are listing tons of items. Other times, items have short descriptions in order to purposefully omit condition issues with the item(s). Make sure that you have the information you need BEFORE bidding on it, especially if the auction would potentially cost you some money. Use the 'Ask Seller' link to get the information you need before you place a bid.

Here is my secret formula to successful EBay bidding. I locate items to bid on, and do not bid early, as we have already discussed. When I am looking for items, I use at least two browser tabs. One is for the EBay listings I am searching. I also have a second tab open to check the value of items. For media items, I use Amazon. It's very easy to search for items in the Amazon marketplace and look at the average price listed for items within the lots that you are looking for during your EBay search. AdAll.com is another location to find values for rare collectible books. If I am searching in collectibles or other EBay categories, I open a second browser tab for searching Completed EBay Listings. I search for the item on the first tab, and then look at the ending prices for similar auctions over the last three months on the second tab.

I generally do not get overly excited about an auction unless I know that there are several individual items that are valuable within the lot. I don't like guessing what items may be hidden in an auction lot. Usually, you can see enough either in the text of the auction's description or by looking at the photographs provided to tell if the lot is worth your time. Watch out for the sneaky seller who sells a large lot of garbage and then throws in one or two valuable items to attract bids. If you only see one or two photos of nice items, but no pictures of the overall lot, or a detailed description of what's in there, look out!

If I can verify that several of the items within the lot will pay for the entire cost of the auction, including shipping, I attempt to win the auction. After a while, you get pretty good at getting a feel for which auctions will also have extra hidden goodies in the lot, besides what was listed or photographed. It's always fun opening your large boxes of goodies to see what you got. Sometimes, you'll have over $100 in extra inventory that you didn't even know about inside your package. Sometimes you only get what was listed in the auction, but, if you did your homework, you should always come out ahead when you re-list the individual items. Plus, you can re-list the remainder of the items that had little value as a lot on EBay, sell it at a garage sale, or donate it to Goodwill for a tax write-off.

GARAGE SALE SHOPPING

Finding stuff to make large profits on at garage sales used to be easy. Now, there are many people re-selling items from garage sales on EBay. Plus, the people holding the garage sales are now more aware of the value of many collectible items than they used to be, so items are priced higher. Still, you can find a lot of great items to sell at sales, often for very cheap prices. Often, you can find $10-20 items for under a dollar. How's that for profit?

Here are a number of tips to help you find stuff at garage sales to sell. Number one, do your homework ahead of time. Go through the newspaper classifieds and Craig's List to find sales that advertise what you like to sell, or similar items. Write down when the sales start and end, and what they are supposed to have at the sale that you are interested in. Look for sales that advertise large bunches of stuff, '25 years of accumulation', or that type of language in the ad.

Make every effort to be at the most attractive sale first when it opens. If you can go to sales on Thursdays and Fridays, you can find much more material to sell than if you wait until the sale has been running for a day or two on Saturday morning. Make yourself a route that hits all of the good sales. This prevents you from wasting time and gas money by going back and forth across the county to get to all of the garage sales. If you can hit a neighborhood or citywide sale, by all means, go there.

Number two, don't waste time fiddle-farting around at sales. Treat your garage sailing as a business. It is fun to find stuff at sales, but you are there for a reason. Say hello to the homeowner and be polite, but don't talk for half an hour. If you get to the tables, and there is obviously only junk there, leave immediately and move on to the next one.

If you do find items that you want to buy, ask if you can stack them by the pay table. Get what you are going to get at the sale, pay, and leave. This allows you to hit the most sales possible in the time that you have for that day.

Number three, look at EVERYTHING at the sale. This may seem to contradict rule number two at first glance, but it really does not. When you get more experienced hitting sales, you will understand exactly what I mean. Don't waste time gabbing, and wandering around, but make sure you look at all the tables at the sale.   I have found tons of great items underneath junk on tables, inside other boxes, scattered in amongst books, in boxes of toys, and everywhere else you can think of. The items you are looking for are items that the seller does NOT know the value of. This stuff could be anywhere at the sale.

As a matter of fact, I have found some of my best items in FREE boxes or 5 or 10 cent boxes, thrown in with a bunch of crud. If you see these types of boxes ALWAYS look in them all the way to the bottom of the box. If it's a free box, you can always grab the whole box to save time, and go through it later. You are doing the homeowner a favor by getting rid of the box of junk for them. Take almost any books, CDs, DVDs, or media items that you see in a free box. I have found multiple $50 books in free boxes at sales.

As a savvy reseller, you also have the advantage of having an Amazon selling account. This puts you ahead of 95% of the re-sellers you are competing with at garage sales, who are only selling on EBay. Look for media items that you can sell for a higher price on Amazon, as well as boxed items with bar codes that you can resell. Make sure you quickly grab anything sealed in shrink wrap that you can sell as New.

Number four may be the most important rule. Make sure that you can sell the items that you are picking up. Condition of the item is one of the most important things to consider when deciding on whether to buy an item. Is the item operational? Does it have all the parts? Does it need additional cords to be usable? Plug electronic items in to test them. Almost everybody has outdoor outlets available to test with. If they refuse to let you test an item, don't buy it. It probably does not work.

Also, keep in mind that some items are valuable without being functional. You just have to remember that you are going to have to spend additional money for parts, plus spend time fixing the item, which cuts into your profit.

For instance, it is quite common to find video game systems without cords, but that does not mean that you should not buy them if the price is right. It is very easy to get cords online for any video game system, and they are usually fairly cheap. You can also save the systems for a while and try to find cords at other sales, or at second-hand stores.

Make sure that you examine the entire item. Does it have broken corners, re-glued pieces, etc.? If it does, the collectible value is going to be significantly reduced.

Also, keep in mind the shipping cost of heavy items. There are many collectible items that would make nice profits, if it weren't for the weight of the item. Figure on all items over one pound to cost over $5 in shipping costs, plus an extra $2+ for every pound after that. A heavy metal item could easy cost your potential winning bidder on EBay an additional $15 in shipping fees on top of their winning bid. Consider the total cost that you think the average collector would pay for an item.

Let's say you found a really cool retro glass lamp that is priced $5 at a garage sale. From your prior research, you have seen comparable lamps priced at about $25 at antique stores. Should you buy this lamp, if it appears operational?

The answer is: You probably will not make much profit on this lamp. The antique shop owner may offer you a slight profit over the $5 that you would be paying for it at the garage sale, but by the time you figure your drive time to the antique store, you won't make much money there. If you had planned on selling the lamp online, remember that the lamp weighs over ten pounds and would cost the potential buyer $15-20 in shipping fees over top of their winning bid.

Large items are also a pain to package, and you have to pay for bubble wrap to prevent damage. So, while the lamp looked like a great item, it probably would be a break-even venture in the long run.

Number five, keep a magnet in your pocket for identifying valuable scrap metals such as copper, brass, and silver-plate. Remember that non-magnetic metals are usually more valuable than the metal objects that stick to your magnet.

RESEARCHING

If there is one area that a motivated seller can stand out above their competition, it is in their knowledge base pertaining to the items that they sell. If I could give fellow sellers one piece of advice, it would be this: Start with what you know, and then broaden your knowledge from there. You really do not have to know much to sell usable items, clothing, and other non-collectible items online. You simply identify the item in an auction or on the Amazon marketplace, describe the condition, and then make it available for purchase.

However, other items such as collectibles, high-end electronics, computer equipment, and auto parts require the seller to have some background knowledge before selling the item. In order to be able to describe the item sufficiently so that a potential buyer is comfortable buying it from you, the seller has to understand what type of information the buyer needs for them to determine value and/or functionality.

Start selling what you are familiar with. If you grew up collecting sports cards and memorabilia, and you have boxes of baseball cards in your closet, start selling your excess cards. You already know how to describe your cards to buyers. You can 'speak the language' to collectors on EBay. You know what an insert card is, and how to identify a rookie card. You know how to describe the condition of the card to a potential buyer.

Get yourself a current price guide for your sports cards so that you have an idea of the current market value. Then, collect a number of cards that you are interested in selling and type the player's name and year of the sport card in the search bar on EBay. Click on the checkbox on the left side of the screen that says 'Completed Listings'. You get a list of the ended auctions from the last three months with your search description. The average ending price is what you should expect to sell your card for, if the condition is also similar.

The same process can be applied to any subject area. When you have an item that you want to determine value on, take a look at the last three months of sales on EBay. You should be able to make a quick determination if the item is worth your time. If you are considering selling the item on Amazon, locate the item in the Amazon marketplace using the search bar, and see what the average price listed is.

EBay completed listings can also help you in other ways. Let's say that you found a vintage Pioneer audio receiver for free at a garage sale. Good for you! Now, how do you make a profit on it, if you have never dealt with electronics before?

If you plug it in and everything works, you just hit the jackpot. Look on the back of the unit and find the model number. Type it into the search bar, and see what similar working units have sold for, and list your receiver starting at the low end of the completed listing's end prices. You want to encourage bidders by starting at what feels like a bargain to the bidder.

If you attempt to test the receiver and it doesn't work at all, don't fret. You actually may make more money by disassembling the receiver and selling the parts. The trick is to determine which components and parts to sell. You should have an idea what parts are going to be sold BEFORE taking the receiver apart, because some larger components are more valuable whole then totally disassembled. For instance, if your vintage audio item has a record player, you will want to keep the entire tone-arm assembly together to sell it.

In order to determine what we are going to sell, we will use Completed Listings again. From the main EBay page, first type in the model number from the receiver. Most of the time, the search will return many whole receivers that were for sale. But, it will also give you a list of parts and components that other sellers have listed and what the ending prices were. For instance, with vintage Pioneer receivers, you would probably find that the outer case was worth listing (and would make you some good money, if it was wood). You would also note that the knobs, feet, emblem, and face plate were worth money. Usually the tuning mechanism, display, and some of the internal workings will also be listed.

You may also want to go to the 'Vintage Electronics' category and look at the Completed Listings for the entire category. This will give you a general idea of some of the parts that are often valuable, regardless of brand. You would probably note that large power transformers are usually worth money, and since your Pioneer has a similar transformer to the ones that you saw in Completed Listings, you would want to list your own transformer in the category that you found the others in.

A good seller is curious. If you are at a garage sale, you should be looking for new sources of income. If you find something interesting, look it up in Completed Listings when you get home, and see if it's worth your time.

I spend a lot of time just browsing Completed Listings in given categories and looking for new areas to list items in. If I find an interesting listing that did really well for another seller, I look at the auction page and try to figure out why it did better than others in the same category. Were there certain words used in the item's title? Were the photos showing a certain aspect of the item? Was the item described in a particular way? If I can pick up anything useful, I use similar wordings in my titles or descriptions.

You may also find totally new areas to sell items in. I remember one night browsing Completed Listings to see if any 1980s-era magazines were worth buying at garage sales, because I was seeing them quite often. I found that 95% of the magazines I was seeing were not going to be worth the time it took to list them. But, I saw some listings in other categories that were interesting.

Other sellers were listing just the advertisements from magazines and newspapers for pretty decent money. Often, the magazines the ads came from could be found for $1, but the ads within could be worth up to $20 apiece. People were looking for ads containing celebrities or certain products (like vintage autos, or Atari 2600 games) and framing them for décor in their homes and businesses.

So I picked up a bunch of magazines, and clipped interesting ads out. I scanned the ads with my scanner, and listed them on EBay. I made several hundred dollars selling magazine ads in a relatively short time. I looked at a number of sellers' listings, and it was apparent that they sold only magazine ads and did quite well.

I sold ads for a while, but I quickly realized that you have to make a lot of listings to make any real money, and I found it quite monotonous clipping and scanning, so I moved on to more interesting ventures. If you are interested in selling ads, there are books available on Amazon for identifying and pricing print ads to get you started. The startup cost is almost zero, and you will make some money if you can find some older magazines to pull ads from.

FREE ITEMS TO SELL: OUTDOORS

DISCLAIMER: Consult the appropriate laws on the collection of goods and materials from government-owned public lands, whether the lands are federal, state, or municipally owned.

There are often laws pertaining to the commercial use of these lands, and the taking and/or use of wild animals, plants, and minerals or their parts may be restricted or forbidden. Vehicle access may also be restricted to certain areas. You can be fined or possibly even arrested for the violation of these laws, so conduct research on the laws BEFORE you enter these lands.

There are thousands of different things that you can find while you are outside doing yard work, recreating, or bee-bopping around in your ORV, snowmobile, or vehicle that you can quickly and easily sell. While you are out having fun, you might as well try to pay for the gas you put in the gas tank to get you out there, right?

Before you leave your house, you should prepare for locating items to sell. Put together a 'gathering kit' that you can bring with you, whether you are in a car or on a smaller recreational vehicle. Find a small gear bag or backpack that is the right size for you to carry, and does not get in the way of the other activities that you got you outside in the first place.

Inside the bag, you will need a lightweight set of tools that you will use often while gathering items to sell. You will want to tailor your set to the types of items that you like to sell. Make sure that you have plenty of room left over inside the bag to place items when you find them.

At the minimum, I would recommend including the following items: Work gloves, bug spray, a small first aid kit, a small magnet, a multi-tool (Leatherman-type) that has both types of screwdrivers, a knife, needle-nose pliers, and a wire cutter; several additional rolled bags i.e. garbage bags or burlap sacks to put stuff in, a map of the area you are exploring, a compass, a cellular telephone, pencil and paper, and this handy-dandy book for reference.

If you have a handheld GPS or smart-phone that has GPS capabilities, you are ahead of the game. You can mark locations to return to, and easily find your way back to your vehicle if you are out on foot.

OK, so after you are mobile, what are you looking for? Basically anything that people might want to use, or that you can find value in. You have already done part of your research by reading this book. You have an excellent selection of items to look for.

Now, just start thinking logically while you are out having fun. When you see things in the woods, either collect them, or write them down on your pad of paper to check when you get home.

When I started this gig, I sat down in front of a computer and just started searching for things that I could possibly find in the woods in my area. I did searches on EBay completed items and Google searches for items I was seeing while hunting, fishing, or whatever else got me outside. Some items were worth gathering, and some were not. Some items I immediately found that I could sell on EBay, some took more digging to find places to sell them.

ORGANIC ITEMS

I remember duck hunting near an abandoned beaver dam, and seeing lots of cool looking beaver-chewed sticks. I wondered if people would use them for rustic home or cabin décor. I grabbed a couple of medium sized logs with nice wood grains, and took them home. I found several areas on EBay where people had sold similar items for décor and animal taxidermy backgrounds. People were also using natural beaver logs with no preparation for crafting candle holders for $2-5 apiece. If you wanted to do some work and either make the candle holders yourself, or power-wash and stain the logs, you could make even more money on each item.

In many areas, local businesses will also pay you to bring them outdoor goods and edible items. Bakeries, delicatessens, restaurants, and specialty shops like organic foods stores may pay good money for things you can easily find and gather such as: berries, nuts, mushrooms, and edible plants like wild asparagus and wild leeks.

If you own wooded property, timber companies may pay you very good money to come to your property and harvest timber. Most timber companies will even do select cutting, where only specific trees are cut, or a stand of trees is thinned. Such a timber harvest is actually very beneficial to the health of the forest and the animals that live there, and any damage to the ground heals naturally in a short time period. Plus, you can receive substantial money for allowing the timber company to harvest on your property.

Similarly, if you own a large tract of land, you may consider contacting an oil and gas company to test your property for mineral harvest. You may be sitting on a gold mine, and don't even know it!

On a smaller scale, many other forest products can be sold to local companies for their resale. Such items would include: Christmas trees, saplings for tree sales, seeds and seed-bearing cones to nurseries for tree regeneration, pine and cedar boughs for wreath making, wood mulch, wood chips, and tree bolts to landscaping companies, and the list goes on and on.

I know several people who make hundreds of dollars every year gathering acorns and other seeds and selling them to tree nurseries, after very little preparation time. You only have to do a little leg work ahead of time and establish a relationship with the managers or owners of these nurseries so that you know what they are buying, and when to bring them your supply to get paid.

MAN-MADE ITEMS

If there is one thing that aggravates me to no end, it is seeing litter in the woods. There should be automatic jail time handed out to any person convicted of littering.

But, there is some nice money to be made on trash found in the woods, or along the roadways. I regularly pick up trash when I find it in the woods or in rivers while I'm recreating. While I'm doing my good deed for the day, I'm also going to see if I can make some money on it, as long as I'm spending my time picking up after others.

First of all, make sure that you wear thick work gloves while handling any man-made materials that you find. There is the potential to be seriously cut, and you could contract a number of diseases by being cut by unclean glass or metal.

I do not open any trash bags found in the woods, and I highly recommend that you do not open any closed bags, either. The health concerns are obvious. You don't know what is in the bag, correct? At the least, you could be dealing with rotten food and diapers. At worst, the contents of a garbage bag could be explosive, if a drug manufacturer threw out the remains of a mobile meth lab!

So, where is the value in discarded litter? You should immediately recognize the intrinsic value of picking up unsightly, environmentally degrading litter in the area where you live. It should make you feel proud to help your community and conserve your local environment by making the effort to pick up that litter. That is the value in picking up most plastics, trash bags, broken glass, shingles, and other litter that has no resale value.

It should not be difficult at all to find a local business or a governmental agency that will allow you to dispose of bags of litter that you selflessly picked up from public land. You should not have to pay to dispose of such materials yourself.

There is also tangible money to be made at these dump sites. I can guarantee you that if 'push came to shove', I could feed my family for months solely off the scrap metal value of litter piles found in the woods on state land where I live. That's not my first choice of material to sell, but it would do just fine in a pinch.

In order to maximize your profit on this scrap metal, consult the chapter on Scrap Metal in this book for the separation and identification of particular metals.

If you have a scrap metal vehicle or trailer, you can continue to add magnetic steel from a number of litter locations until you get a full load to sell at the scrap yard. If you do not have a designated vehicle, you may opt to mark scrap metal spots on a map or GPS unit, until you think that you would have enough steel to make a load, and then pick them all up in the same trip.

Remember to remove anything that is not magnetic (non-ferrous) from the scrap metal, before going to the scrap dealer. Anything that is non-ferrous should be sold separately as it has worth significantly more value than ferrous steel.

And now, for the real money. As you are loading your scrap metal, remove any items with dedicated recyclable value. One example would be aluminum beverage cans in states with deposit laws. There are also many other items with designated values listed in APPENDIX C, such as cellular telephones, Lithium-Ion Batteries, and printer cartridges.

Next, look to see if there is anything that you can sell individually. Look for any media items, like music CDs, DVDs, video games and books that are in good enough shape to sell.

One of my best finds ever was in a trash pile along a road on state land. I stopped to pick up the litter, and noticed a huge pile of 1980s heavy metal CDs that had been tossed out with the litter. Many of the cases and paperwork therein were destroyed by the elements, but 90% of the CDs themselves were just fine. I listed over 100 of the CDs on Amazon, with values of up to $20 each. I sold most of them within two months! There was also a working video game system worth $50 in the pile. Of course, I also disposed of the rest of the litter that was there. Intrinsic value, folks.

You should also look for board games, handheld video games, and electronics to sell for parts, collectibles, vintage bottles, batteries, battery chargers, computers, cords, remote controls, and other similar items.

Check inside anything with a battery compartment for batteries. I have found many usable alkaline batteries lying around inside litter piles. You can also save the battery compartment doors to sell on commonly owned items like remote controls and toys. Save any rechargeable batteries as well. You can make very good money on large rechargeable batteries, if they are not completely dead. Even if you don't have the manufactured charger, it is still possible to recharge most batteries. I will provide you with a link later in this document that provides directions on how to recharge many supposedly 'dead' batteries, and save yourself $20-50 on each battery.

After you have removed all of the items that you can sell individually and the recyclable items, hit all of the metal with your magnet. Take anything out of the pile that is non- ferrous. Make sure you remove any copper wires and cords. Make a separate pile for this material, or put it in a large sturdy bag. Also include in this pile any junk electronics that you plan on disassembling for sellable parts, or the interior copper and precious metals content.

Finally, remove the large steel frames from any furniture that is there. Items like sleeper sofas can have $10-15 in steel in their frames alone. Put the remaining ferrous metal in your scrap vehicle, separate from your non-ferrous pile. Take your valuable non-ferrous pile, bag it, and remove it. Complete your work by bagging the rest of the litter and disposing of it on the way to scrap metal dealer.

In addition to piles of litter, there are many other free single items that can be found while outside that you can sell. Along roadways you can find hubcaps and wheel rims worth $2-3 each at the scrap metal dealer, recyclable cans, bungee straps, ratchet straps, and if you are really luck, exhaust pipes with the platinum-containing catalytic converters attached. Junk 'Cats' are worth $40-150 each, due to the platinum content inside them!

If you can find a junk vehicle in the woods, congratulations! You can haul the body to the scrap dealer for at least $200, if you can get it out of the woods. If you can't get the car out, you may very well be able to strip out a bunch of parts to sell individually on EBay. You can also remove the 'cat' from newer vehicles, take all of the copper wires, remove the radio, etc. If it is an older vehicle and not too rusted, you may be able to sell the chrome trim, decals, hood ornaments and other collectible items for very good money.

Some other man-made items that I have found and sold or converted to personal use while outdoors are: vintage fishing lures and tackle, golf clubs, golf balls, railroad ties, railroad spikes, lumber, automobile batteries (why would you throw these out? You get at least $5 just by taking them to Wal-Mart!), tools, doors, door knobs, bench seats, coolers, bottles, vintage cans, winter outerwear, a paintball helmet, copper pipes, tents, hunting blinds, ice spuds, duck decoys, duck decoy anchors, shotgun shell hulls, brass shell casings, vintage shotgun shell boxes, can openers, collectible lighters, folding chairs, camp chairs, working radios, Walkman radios, an I-pod, and on and on.

For a complete list of free outdoor items that you can sell and where to sell them, see the Outdoors Items Appendix provided with this document.

SELLING SCRAP METAL: EASIEST MONEY YOU'LL EVER MAKE

I wish I could go back in time. If I could transport myself back to when I was a teenager, with the knowledge I have now about selling scrap metal, I could have saved myself several summers of misery working at the local grocery store. I could have been working outside at my own pace, and made twice as much money as I did bagging groceries and dealing with snobby tourists.

Finding and selling scrap metal is extremely easy, not very competitive, and you can do it anywhere. You can start collecting scrap for free, and you do not need a large area to collect it in. Plus, there is good money to be made in selling scrap.

In addition, you are cleaning up the environment by picking up metal that would otherwise take decades to biodegrade. You are keeping materials that you can make money on from being taken to landfills, and we have all heard that many landfills are completely full already.

So why doesn't everybody sell scrap metal, if it is so easy to make money on? Good question. I think that there are several things that keep the majority of people away. Many people seem to think that you have to be a scientist to identify different types of metals, and that selling to a scrap metal dealer is a mysterious process that requires extensive training to be able to complete.

This could not be further from the truth. You need absolutely no prior knowledge of metals to sell scrap. Selling scrap metal can be as simple as this:

Find metal objects, throw them into a truck, transport the metal to the scrap metal dealer, drive your truck onto their scales just as you would pull into a drive-through car wash, unload the metal from your truck where they tell you to, re-weigh your truck, and go into the dealer to get paid. The whole process can be completed in twenty minutes for a pick-up sized load.   It is extremely easy, and you do not even have to know what type of metal you have. Of course, you will make much more money once you know how to separate your metals, but that is easily accomplished, too.

I also think that there is the perception that selling scrap would take up a lot of room on one's property, and that scrapping is a messy business. Well, that may be true if you are a large-scale scrapping outfit, but you can contain a modest scrap metal venture in a very small area.

I got into selling scrap as a way to minimize the loss on metal items that I had bought at garage sales with the intention of selling on EBay, but ended up not being able to sell. I was also picking up litter from the woods and looking for someplace to take the metal so that I did not have to throw it in the trash.

Initially, I just started throwing all of the metal into the bed of my plow truck, which I only used in the winter.   The first time I emptied the truck out at the scrap metal dealer, I made $160, selling all types of metals together as 'Tin', which is how most scrap metal dealers classify loads of metal that are unprocessed.

Later, I did more research on scrapping, and found out that I could have made an extra $50 by selling the aluminum objects separate from the rest of the load. But hey, I was pretty happy at the time, making $160 on a bunch of junk.

GETTING STARTED

You can start collecting scrap without spending any money at all. All you need is a small area to collect metal in, some large boxes or bins, heavy work gloves, the tool kit described in the Outdoors section of this book, a magnet, and a vehicle or trailer to haul the metal to the scrap dealer in. Bolt cutters and a hacksaw come in handy, as well.

This chapter is intended to be a very general guide to the art of scrapping. After reading this chapter, you should feel very comfortable with the process of selling scrap metal. You will understand the basics of how to separate metal, and where to go online to increase your knowledge base. It is not a complete how-to manual for starting a scrap metal business. You will still need to broaden your knowledge of metals through experience and your own research.

Selling scrap metal is one area in which people with very little spare time can save themselves and their family significant money. Even if you do not want to commit the time and effort into starting a second business using the other information in this book, you should strongly consider selling scrap metal. You could easily save enough metal to sell once a year and pay for all of the Christmas presents for your family! Simply saving the steel and aluminum food cans (Just rinse them out and remove the paper labels) and metal lids from jars for a year could easily yield over $100 at the scrap metal dealer. Now if you could get your neighbors to save theirs, too, you are on your way to a nice side job.

THE BASICS OF SCRAPPING

You have to realize that the scrap metal business works just like any other business. The metal itself has a value, which is similar to stock prices. The value is called a spot price. The spot price of each particular type of metal fluctuates, depending on supply and demand for that metal across large regions of the country and the world. The spot prices for each type of metal can be found at any time on the internet.

The spot price is the only point in the scrap selling process that has a fixed value. Everything else is determined by individual scrap metal dealers. To illustrate this, let's say that you have a load of shiny aluminum to sell. You check online, and see that the spot price for Aluminum is $0.85/LB. Should you expect to be paid $0.85/LB when you go to your local scrap dealer? Of course not.

The spot price is quoted for clean processed aluminum. You have used manufactured aluminum. The dealer you are selling it to is a middle-man. He has to buy your metal, and then negotiate a better price with the larger metal processing company that he sells to in order to make a profit.

What does that mean for you? Number one, you will never sell your scrap metal at the spot price, but it gives you a good indicator of whether the metal's value is rising or falling. Try to sell when the spot price is rising, not at the bottom of a price fall.

Number two, the prices quoted to you at a scrap metal dealer are not etched in stone and they are not the same at all scrap metal dealers in your area.

The easy comparison is to gas stations. Not all of the gas stations in your area will charge the same price for a gallon of unleaded gas, but they will almost always be in the same ball park because of the overriding oil prices.

The difference between metal and gas is that sometimes if you contact the scrap metal dealer ahead of time, the buy price can be adjusted, if you have a large load of a particular type of metal. At the very least, you may want to check around to see which scrap dealer has the best buy price for the metal you are going to be selling before you decide where to take your scrap.

Before you even start scrapping, you should go to a Metal Spot Price internet page and take a look at the values of the common metals that you will be finding. You should know which metals are more valuable, so that you can look for them.

SEPARATING METALS

The easiest way to increase your profits in the scrapping business is to correctly identify and separate the more valuable non-ferrous (non-magnetic) metals from the more commonly found ferrous metals, such as steel.

Let's revisit the load of metal that we sold at the beginning of this chapter. $160 is not bad for a load of junk metal. But, if you are going to make the effort to save the metal and haul it to the scrap dealer, you may as well get the maximum value for it.

You will want to sell loads of one particular classification of metal whenever possible, instead of half-full loads, or mixed metal loads. At the very least, you will want to remove the non-ferrous metal from the steel. Steel will get you about $240 a ton, or about 12 cents a pound. Shiny Aluminum can be sold for over 45 cents a pound, and bare copper wires can be sold for over $2.50 a pound.

Copper and aluminum can often be found inside large metal items, such as appliances. You can usually remove the more valuable metals in several minutes, making it well worth your time to do so.

So how do I tell the different types of metal apart, you may ask. There are many ways to identify metals, but the easiest method to separate metals is to use the visible characteristics of the metals. If the metal is not silver colored, remove it from the rest of the scrap. Non-silver metals would include copper, brass, bronze, gold (if you are lucky), and their alloys. All of these metals are worth removing and collecting separately.

For similarly colored metals, there are several ways to further distinguish them. The first way is to check the metal object with a magnet. This is particularly helpful for separating non-magnetic stainless steel and thick aluminum from common magnetic steel. A magnet will also tell you if a copper colored metal item is pure copper or an alloy, which is worth much less.

Another easy way to separate metals is by their weight. Lead items are extremely dense and very heavy. Steel items are also relatively heavy. Aluminum, on the other hand, is fairly light compared to say, non-ferrous Stainless steel. Shiny aluminum and non-ferrous Stainless can be difficult to differentiate for beginners.

A third way you can tell metals apart is with a 'spark test'. This method sounds more difficult than the other two methods, but really is quite easy. All it involves is hitting your metal with a rotary tool (Dremel) with a cutting wheel. This is extremely helpful for differentiating stainless steel and thick aluminum. Steel sparks, aluminum does not. You can also identify several high value metal carbides with a spark test.

Once you start separating the different types of metals, you will quickly become proficient at the task, and you will often be able to tell what type of metal an object is made just by looking at it, or feeling the weight of it.

A TRIP TO THE SCRAP METAL DEALER

As I alluded to earlier, one reason many people do not sell scrap metal is because they are unfamiliar with the process of selling metal to a dealer. I believe that after reading this chapter, you will feel confident enough to go to the scrap dealer on your own for the first time.

I will go over a typical trip to the metal dealer. You will see that there really is nothing difficult about the process. The only thing that is difficult at all is loading the heavy metal into your truck or trailer.

The first thing that you must do is take an inventory of all of your collected scrap metal. Every trip that you make to the scrap yard costs you gas money and time, so minimize the number of trips, if at all possible.

You should already have your metals separated ahead of time. Usually, when I go to the scrap dealer to sell scrap, I have a pickup bed-load of steel. Put as much metal into the bed of you truck as possible, and then use ratchet straps or tie-downs to secure your load.

It's illegal to transport large loads without securing them, and it is also dangerous for you and other motorists.

You may also have enough aluminum to fill a small trailer. If so, you can bring the trailer with you and save yourself a trip. Make sure to secure your load, just as you did with the scrap in your truck bed.

I usually have some non-ferrous scrap to sell, as well. That is where the real money is. You can pack up the inside of your vehicle with boxes of copper, brass, small amounts of aluminum, and other separated non-ferrous metals.

For those people without access to pickup trucks or trailers, you will probably only be selling non-ferrous metals, as the ferrous metals are not going to be worth your time. You cannot transport enough volume of non-ferrous metal to make the trips worthwhile.

The only thing that you really have to prepare for is the unloading of the metal at the scrap yard. Make sure that you have your non-ferrous separated, and placed in either heavy bags or sturdy boxes, so that it is easy to handle when you unload at the scrap yard.

Before you leave, check all of your tie-downs, check the tires on your vehicle and trailer, and the fluids in your vehicle. You may be hauling more weight than what your vehicle is used to, if you do not normally work your vehicles hard. It's OK if your vehicle looks like the truck from the TV show 'Sanford & Son' when you're ready to go. It is not supposed to look pretty.

Make sure that you have a pair of heavy work gloves, work clothes, and possibly a flat shovel for scooping loose metal pieces from your truck or trailer. It also doesn't hurt to have a hammer and crowbar, because sometimes large metal pieces will get wedged together and you will have to separate them.

When you arrive at the scrap yard, there will be an office building with a set of drive-on scales nearby, at the front of the property. Pull off of the road, and go into the office. Make sure that you have your wallet or purse with you.

Go to the main desk, and tell the attendant that you have scrap metal to sell. You will provide your identification, or the attendant may ask you for personal information, address, etc. This information is provided to prevent criminals from illegally selling stolen copper pipes and other high-end metals to scrap yards, and also is used to issue your check when your trip is complete.

The attendant will usually ask you whether you have non-ferrous metals to sell. The attendant will hand you a ticket or sheet of paper with your information on it, and send you back to your vehicle.

If you have non-ferrous metal to sell (which you should), you may be instructed to go to the non-ferrous unloading area first. When you get to the specified location, you will unload your boxes or bags of separated non-ferrous metals one material at a time. Each material will be weighed on a foot scale inside, and then you will deposit the material where the employee tells you to place it. The employee keeps track of the weight of the materials you brought. When you are done dropping off all of your non-ferrous metals, the employee will give his list of weights and materials to the main office for calculation. You may also receive a copy. This process takes only several minutes.

Next, you will sell your ferrous metals, which is usually steel, or mixed metal which is sold as 'Tin', or 'Unprocessed'. Pull your vehicle onto the main scale near the office building. There will be a large metal area on the scale, where you will center the weight of your load. Usually there is a set of lights that resemble traffic lights near the window of the office building. The attendant inside the office will look out the window at your vehicle. Once it is positioned correctly and the weight from the scale has been recorded, the light will change colors, and you will proceed through the scales and into the main scrap yard.

Usually within sight of the scales, there will be another employee waiting for you. He or she will take a look at your load, and determine what type of material you have for the payment calculation. Hopefully, you have separated your metal, so that your payment is not calculated using the 'unprocessed' rate, as you will be losing significant money.

The employee will make a note on your ticket about the contents of your load, and then he or she will direct you where to dump. If you have all steel, you will be sent to an area where a large magnet will pick up the majority of the metal.

If you have a mixed load, or a bed cap or something else that prevents the magnet from unloading your metal, you will be directed to another unloading area. You will manually unload your metal into a large pile of metal objects. I always have to unload manually, as my truck has a contractor's rack over the bed. I unload my metal in about ten or fifteen minutes, it is not a big deal.

After you are unloaded, you head back to the front of the yard, re-weigh your empty truck on the same set of scales that you first weighed your load on, and then go back into the main office.

Hand the attendant your ticket. He or she will calculate all of your metals sold, and issue you a check for the full amount. It is as easy as that. The entire process should take you about half an hour, unless you have to wait in line to unload, which happens quite often.

I have been to a number of scrap yards, and the process is very similar at each one. If you have an additional trailer, you may have to go through the scales twice. The scrap yard may reverse the order of dropping of ferrous and non-ferrous metals. Other than that, things will go pretty much as I explained in this chapter.

PRECIOUS METALS: FAST, EASY MONEY

When most people think of selling scrap metal, they picture the loaded down pick-up trucks traveling down the highway with pieces of steel sticking out haphazardly from the overflowing bed. This is also where a lot of scrappers make their grocery money.

However, the real difference between the average scrapper and the successful businessperson is in their knowledge of the craft. Anybody can throw a bunch of junk into their trailer and make a couple of extra dollars, but the experienced scrapper knows that the real money in the scrap metal business is made in selling precious metals, such as gold, silver, and platinum.

Often, these precious metals, which can be valued at up to $1580 an ounce, can be found within larger pieces of machinery that is scrapped at the base scrap steel rate of near ten cents a pound!

Of course these precious metals are found in relatively meager amounts in these places, but it does not take much volume to net you a nice profit. The trick is to know where to locate the precious metals within the larger pieces of machinery. You have to do your research.

The easiest of the precious metals to find is copper (usually considered semi-precious). Almost all machinery and motors have copper inside them, due to copper's conductive properties. 95% of the wires you find will have copper inside them. Whenever you find copper, it is worth saving. Copper has a current spot price of $3.60 a pound. Even copper that is sealed inside motors and transformers can be sold at significantly increased rates over their base metals by selling it as copper breakage. Most scrap metal dealers will have a set rate for copper breakage, or electric motors, which currently sells for about thirty cents a pound, or three times more than scrap steel.

I remember the first time I took a load of scrap to the scrap metal yard. I had a truck bed overloaded with steel, and several large boxes of stripped copper. I was very surprised when the boxes of copper netted me almost as much money as the truck bed full of steel.

Again, copper is very easy to find. Start by saving all of the power cords that you see. If you see electrical items for free at garage sales, you should at least be saving the power cords for scrap copper. If something breaks or stops working in your home, cut the power cord off and save it. You should also disassemble appliances for interior copper and other precious metals.

The question often arises, as to whether the thrifty scrapper is further ahead to simply throw copper wires into a box and sell it as insulated copper, or to strip the insulation off and get the higher value for the non-insulated 'clean' copper. After doing a fair amount of research, the consensus seems to be that standard house wires and similar sized wires should be sold as insulated copper wires. Larger wires that would qualify as #1 copper should be stripped and sold as clean copper. Generally, #1 copper is considered to be any bare wire that is larger than a standard No.2 pencil lead and has a single layer of insulation. Anything smaller than that is #2 copper. #3 copper is telephone wires and computer cables.

Of course, if you have lots of spare time, feel free to make the extra profit and strip insulation to your heart's content, but remember - time is money.

Decorative solid copper items and copper tubing can also be found rather routinely at sales and thrift shops. Remember to keep your magnet with you. Non-magnetic clean copper can be sold for about $3 a pound. Non-magnetic copper coated ferrous metals are sold as copper breakage - thirty cents a pound.

You can also find gold and silver within the metal appliances and electronic scrap that you find discarded in various locations. This is where you can really make some extra dough. Silver currently spots at over $29 a troy ounce and gold sells for over $1580 a troy ounce. It does not take much gold or silver to make some nice money.

Where can I find this gold and silver, you may ask? Ah.. That is question, isn't it? There is a ton of information on locating scrap silver and gold on the internet. Several very good links have been provided for you in the free internet links at the end of this document.

To make a long story short, there are several locations where you can consistently find silver and gold in electronics and machinery. Computers have a fair amount of gold in the fingers on the connectors of the circuit boards, and also within the CPU processor chips. The older the computer is, the higher the gold content it will have inside it, in most cases. Some of the older circuit boards are actually gold plated.

Another good place to find silver and gold is in electrical contacts. While these contacts are often small and worth only 25 cents to a dollar, some silver contacts in vintage industrial machinery can be worth $20 a piece. I have found solid silver contacts in 1950s industrial lifts that weighed almost two ounces, or over $50 a piece!

This can be to your advantage, because a lot of the free electronics and machinery you are going to find are going to be old rusty vintage items. It is quite common to find 1950s or 60s electrical junk laying there in the woods, waiting for you to it home and disassemble it.

Some other common places to find gold and silver is in thin interior wires in vintage electronics, some gold faced diodes in computers, vintage rotary telephone and telecommunications items, vintage video game systems, and inside cellular telephones. I have provided an excellent link for several publications that I have bought and picked up a tremendous amount of information from, regarding the harvest of gold, silver and platinum from electronics, dental scrap, and other sources. I highly recommend that you check them out in the links at the end of the document.

You can also find gold and silver quite regularly at sales and thrift shops, once you know what you are looking for. You would be surprised at how many sterling silver items that you can find at thrift shops once you get a knowledge base and start looking for them. Many of the people that price the items in thrift shops do not use current spot prices to price with, and you can often get a great bargain just by knowing the spot price and how to identify different types of precious metals.

There are many books and internet pages devoted to identifying gold and silver in its different forms, and also how to evaluate the gold content by using scratch-tests and strike sets.   By all means, please take the time to research in this area while you are reading about how to find "Almost Free" items.

This book is devoted to locating free or almost free sources of income. You will not find "karat" gold or sterling silver items very often for cheap, but if you have done your homework, it is very possible to buy these items and resell them for a nice profit, so do your reading on this subject.   What we are going to discuss in this book is where to find gold and silver for free! Yes, that's right. I have found hundreds of dollars' worth of gold and silver just lying around in the woods and in junk piles, just waiting to be reclaimed. Does it have the romance of panning for gold in a mountain stream Out West? No, it doesn't. But the value is the same - gold is gold, plain and simple.

Where do we find this free gold and silver, you ask? Well, it's all around you. Gold and silver are among the most conductive of metals, which make them highly useful in a wide array of electronics and machinery. Gold and silver also are very resistant to abrasion and they do not oxidize (rust), which makes them the primary metals used in electronic contact points, and shiny surface coating for decorative items.

What is most important in locating gold and silver is understanding where it has been used. This is accomplished through diligent research, including the reading of this book.

Remember, it does not take much gold or silver material to add up to significant profits. If you can collect enough gold plated items or gold contacts to add up to one troy ounce of gold, then you have "mined" enough material to equal seven or eight large truck-loads of scrap steel! Gold currently spot-prices at close to $1620 a troy ounce. Silver, which is used more than gold, prices at close to $30 an ounce.

The historical price of gold is also important to understand (and silver historically parallels the gold price). The price of gold per ounce stayed fairly constant at between $35-40 from 1935 all the way up until 1971, when the US Dollar was removed from the Gold Standard. After 1971, the price of gold jumped from $40 an ounce to $150 an ounce by 1974, and then up to $615 by 1980. Do you think there's going to be a difference in how much gold was plated onto costume jewelry, gold rimmed plates, and eyeglass frames in 1968 when gold was $35 an ounce compared to 1995, when gold was $380 dollars an ounce? You betcha.

Even throughout the 1980s and 90s, gold stayed fairly steady at between $350 and $400, except for a spike in prices in the year 1980, when gold hit $615 an ounce. It wasn't until 2005 that the price of gold really skyrocketed. So, there is still significant gold to be found in items that are not all that old, relatively speaking.

That being said, the PRIME decade for finding the most gold and silver in electronics and decorations is from about 1961 to 1971. This is the time period when gold and silver had the most uses, and electronics from the era were often heavily plated with silver, and sometimes gold. Manufacturers were much more lenient in the application of gold and silver - remember, gold was only $35 an ounce, compared to over $1500 an ounce today.

It is common to find electronics from the 1960s for next to nothing at garage sales, thrift stores, or even laying in junk heaps. I guarantee you that there are thousands of these items in landfills near you right now. The electronics from the 60s are now over fifty years old – most of these items are broken, missing pieces, or downright outdated. A few are collector's items, but most are heavy, bulky clunkers that take up too much room in people's homes. Their loss is your gain.

Any time you see electronics for free, you should be grabbing and running. This is especially true, if they are from 1960-1985, or so. Not only do electronics from that era contain more gold than newer models, their interior components are also more valuable to sell on EBay, as we have discussed earlier.

WHERE TO FIND GOLD FOR CHEAP

We all know about the traditional methods of finding gold, including strip mining, gold panning, and dredging. All of them involve back-breaking labor and lots of money invested in order to get to the gold.

Why go through all this effort when there is gold to be found above ground for very little cost? We are going to talk about some specific items that you can find at garage sales, thrift stores, and in scrap piles for free.

First of all, look for scrap or discarded computers from the 1980s and 90s. You can find these computers for next to nothing. I have found quite a few computers in free boxes at sales and lying in the woods. They all have gold and silver inside, it is only a question of how much.

First, almost all motherboards contain gold in the connector fingers. Motherboards are the main circuit board inside the computer, and they will also have a heat sink with an IC chip underneath. The IC chip will also contain a significant amount of gold, and sometimes can be worth more than the spot gold value because of the collectible market of these chips to 'techies'. Check your EBay completed listings to see if the IC chip is worth more as a collectible piece.

Some of the older personal computers can have circuit boards that are completely lined with plated gold, and many of the connectors within the circuit boards also contain gold. Communications devices and high-tech items from the 1980s can also contain similar boards.

The circuit boards inside back planes and hard drives in computers also contain gold and silver in small amounts. These items are often more valuable sold as whole units than disassembled into smaller parts. The same is also true of RAM, or computer memory boards, which also contain small gold fingers. RAM is almost always more valuable when sold as whole boards than when the gold fingers are trimmed off of the boards. The smaller wires and the connector jacks that connect the wires to the circuit boards also often have gold or silver inside them.

Platinum can also be found in minute amounts in the platters of hard drives inside computers. These items can be saved and sold in large lots.

Gold can also be found inside of almost every cellular telephone. Some of the early cell phones can actually have a significant amount of gold in their circuitry, and these are the ones that you can find in junk piles and free boxes. All cell phones are worth money. If you see them, pick them up. If nothing else, there are many internet sites that offer a set price for scrap phones, dead or alive, so they are worth your time to pick them up.

Newer printer cartridges also contain gold in their contact buttons, which is why they also have a set scrap value on a number of internet sites.

There are many vintage items from the 60s and 70s that actually contain a fair amount of gold. Almost every item with a circuit board has gold or silver contacts. Some of the high- end electronics have large gold contacts. I once found a large factory loader from the 1960s that had interior gold contacts that added up to over ¼ ounce of pure gold, which is worth over $375 in today's gold market!

I have found that the 1960s audio equipment, including turntables, consoles, and radios will occasionally have silver coated copper wires throughout the entire main circuit board. These wires are always worth saving for precious metal refining. Almost all of these vintage audio items also have gold and silver contacts, and also have a fair amount of copper wiring inside.

Rotary telephones from the 1960s - early 1980s contain gold in their mouth pieces, and in several other internal contacts. The jacks of almost all telephones contain small amounts of gold inside the connectors.

There also many vintage items that you can find small amounts of gold in, where you would not expect to find gold. Such items would include: Some cologne and perfume caps, designer pens and pen holders, older trophies, dental work, lamps and lamp shades, gold colored trim in band uniforms and Rotary and Lions Club hats, Gold-trimmed china and dishes, picture frames, purse trim, lapel pins, clocks, cigarette holders, cuff-links, eyeglass frames, plaques, emblems, calculators, all switches, plug ends, telephone key pads, ribbon connectors, thermostatic contacts from high temperature items like popcorn poppers and electric skillets, coasters, waste baskets, vintage clothes gold-colored trim, coffee cups, and many more locations. If the item looks like it may possibly be gold, test it with your gold tester!

1950s and 60s gold-colored lamps are fairly easy to find in thrift stores, as they are large by today's standards, and therefore sell slowly. Some of the these large lamps have a fair amount of gold plating in their bases, well worth the asking price at thrift stores, which is often $1-2.

There are many places that you can find items with interior components that you can sell, or scrap for metal value. You just have to use some ingenuity. Besides finding items set out for free or discarded in the woods, you can also get these items for free by doing some leg-work. Think about where these items are going to show up.

Where do items that do not sell at garage sales go when the sales wrap up? In the garbage? Why not make yourself some business cards and give them to garage sales holders. Tell them you will haul away all their unsold items for free after the sale ends. You are going to get some junk, and you may need access to a dumpster, but you will get a lot of good scrap metal and other items that we have discussed.   For large sales, you may even get paid a nominal fee to haul stuff away.

You can also make a classified ad or Craig's List ad that offers your services for removal of appliances, electronics and other items.   You could visit second-hand stores and antique shops and ask the manager if you could leave a large box for them to put broken or unsold vintage electronics, gold and silver plated items, etc. You may have a pay a small fee for each box-full of items, but probably not. Just start thinking where dead electronics and appliances may be found, and you will come up with more ideas on your own.

WHAT TO DO WITH YOUR GOLD AND SILVER CONTACTS

There are many investors looking to take advantage of the security of investing in gold and silver. The risk is considerably less than speculating on the stock market. Gold and silver are commodities with a finite supply. It is getting harder and harder to find, so the spot price is going to continue to trend upward over time.

The question for many gold and silver scrappers is: Do I save the scrap gold and silver and cash in several years after the gold prices advance, or do I cash in my gold immediately?

I have been saving my gold for several years now. I think that it's going to be a nice little kitty in several years, when our family is going to be paying for college tuitions.

However, you may opt to cash in your gold, silver and platinum as you collect it. This can be accomplished in several ways.

First, you can send all of your contacts to an internet precious metals company, such as those listed in the Appendices in the back of the book. Keep in mind that if you sell your scrap gold to these companies, you will have to subtract your shipping costs in getting your gold to their location, and rely on their processes for evaluating the gold.

You can also take you contacts to a physical assayer or gold buyer in your area. They will assess the value of your gold or silver, and issue you a check for the value on site.

The third avenue for your consideration is more risky, but also will yield the highest value for your scrap precious metals. If you can effectively refine your own metal, you cut out several "middle-men", and get the most value from your hard work.

You must consider that the refining of precious metals is a somewhat risky business for beginners. The refining processes require the use of caustic materials, including acids. They also take some time and effort, and you will have to purchase chemicals and hardware to complete the refining.

If you choose to take this route, you do so at your own risk. Refining precious metals can emit noxious vapors and the acids can cause severe burns. You must have a secure area in which to refine, where you have ventilation system and can keep children away from. This is not a suggestion. It is necessity! There are many different methods for refining precious metals, and I have not tried any of them, opting instead to hoard my gold and silver, with the goal of selling to a reputable precious metal buyer in the future. I do not recommend any one method of refinery.

There are many different methods for refining precious metals, which can be found online through your research. Websites for refining gold and silver from electronic scrap can be found in the 'Links' at the end of the document.

NOTES ON PRECIOUS METALS IN COINS

Quickly answer the following question: How much is a U.S. Quarter Dollar worth? Twenty-five cents, you say? Not so fast, my friend.

The average person walking down the street will tell you that a quarter is a quarter. They are all worth twenty-five cents. That is true, if you are spending the quarter in a store. But, if you are a knowledgeable investor, that quarter is currently worth $5.23 if it is from 1963 or before, due to the metal composition of the coin.

All quarters minted before 1964 contain 90% silver. The same is true of dimes from the same period. Even war nickels minted from 1942-45 contain 35% silver, and are worth $1.35 at today's melt value. For a complete list of melt values for circulated coins, check the Links at the end of this document.

90% silver coins are tough to find on the street. Consider yourself very lucky if you receive a silver coin as change in a payment transaction. There are not many of these left in circulation, due to many people knowing the value of the silver contained in the coins. That being said, there is nothing wrong with checking your piggy bank to see if there's some silver in there!

The melt value also gives you a reference point, so that you can determine if you want to buy silver coins if you find them at flea markets, antique stores, or garage sales (rarely). Many antique store owners do not frequently update their prices, and the silver spot price can shoot up from time to time, allowing you to pick up silver below the spot price.

Even if the silver is priced at spot, you may elect to buy the coins, and save them to sell when the spot price rises. Silver and gold are very dependable investment options; much safer than stocks. There is only so much metal that is left to be mined or reclaimed. The price is going to go up eventually. It's only a matter of when, and how much.

Silver coins can be hard to find at an affordable price, but one coin that you can easily find that has a definitive spot price is copper pennies.

I remember researching scrap metals on EBay, and seeing people buying bag fulls of pennies. I was intrigued. Why are people buying pennies when they are only worth one cent?

Then, I thought about it a little more. It's all about volume and investment. All U.S. pennies minted before 1986, and Canadian pennies minted before 1994 are made of 95% copper. A 1980 Lincoln penny is currently worth almost three cents in melt value, although it is illegal to melt the coins down for copper (it is NOT illegal to melt down old silver coins, for some reason). Regardless, the coins still contain a specified amount of copper, and are traded based on that value. The value of copper is also on the rise.

Start saving your old pennies. Ten years from now you will be glad that you did.

NOTES ON SATELLITE DISHES & RECEIVERS

A person could make a nice side-job business by offering to remove unsightly decaying satellite dishes from people's yards for a nominal fee, or for free, if that does not work.   You can also stop at homes that have these old dishes, and offer your service in removing them. Many people will be appreciative to you for cleaning up their yards or homes.

Start looking for these old outdated, non-functioning satellite dishes and you will see them everywhere. Look for the huge 3-4' wide mesh dishes from the 1980s and early 90s. None of the systems that these dishes were designed for are in use anymore. Also look for the older model DIRECTV and Dish Network dishes. They will usually be sun faded and/or have green mildew or moisture marks on them.

Many of them are even on ground level, so you don't have to mess with climbing ladders and getting on roofs.   People don't have any use for them anymore, but they do not want to take the time or make the effort to remove them.

This is great for you.   You can remove dishes on ground level in about fifteen minutes. All you have to do is cut the pole off and throw the whole pole and dish into your truck and you are done. Disassemble the dish from the pole later at your facility.

Cut the sod or turf in a circle around the hole and attempt to save the grass for when you are done. Dig down about 8" around the base of the pole. Make the hole wide enough to get a reciprocating or cut-off saw (or a hacksaw, if you don't have access to a cut-off saw) into. Cut the pole off level with the ground. Trim any cords that are showing. Put a small board over the stump of the pole, so it does accidentally cut someone's feet if it gets dug up. Cover the board with dirt level with the yard. Replace the sod, if you were successful in saving it. If not, you may elect to carry a small bag of grass seed with you to fix the hole that you made.

You should also ask the resident there is they have the receiver box or remote control for the dish that you removed for them. The receivers contain large circuit boards that you can harvest precious metals from. The remote controls also have small boards inside.

Why go through the hassle of removing dishes? Gold. There is gold and silver in all satellite transponders, and there is quite a bit in the older large dishes, and even the first generation DirecTV dishes. The transponder is the plastic piece in the center of the dish that receives the signal from the satellite itself. The dish itself is also usually magnetic stainless and if you have a good number of these, you can get a higher rate for the stainless than normal shred value for steel.

But, back to the gold. I just opened up several transponders from vintage dishes to see what was inside them. I was surprised to find that the entire circuit boards inside several transponders were plated in gold, and there were several other interior components that had gold in them too. The circuitry also was lined with silver. The jacks were brass, with gold pins.

To get at the interior circuit boards, hit the seam on the transponder with a hammer to split it open. The circuit board comes out very easily.

SELLING SCRAP METAL ON EBAY

It is easy and profitable to sell scrap metal on eBay. I will go through this process, as I did for selling metal at a scrap yard.

First, go onto the USPS website and order yourself a selection of Priority Mail shipping boxes. All of these boxes are free to order, and have no shipping charges. The USPS wants customers shipping items by Priority Mail, as it makes them more money than the same items shipped Parcel Post or First Class Mail.

Get a variety of sizes of boxes, but make sure that you get the large regular Priority Mail and Large Flat Rate Priority Mail boxes, plus some smaller regular Priority Mail and Medium Flat Rate boxes.   Once you get the boxes, start collecting your scrap metal in the Large Flat Rate Boxes, especially solid metal copper and brass. The copper box will probably contain copper pipes, ornamental copper items, and copper connectors, etc. The brass box could have ornamental brass objects, brass bullet casings, plumbing fixtures, etc.

Once you fill up a Flat Rate box with one type of scrap, you are ready to sell it on eBay. Weigh your box with the metal contents inside it on a scale with a digital read-out.   Take a digital photo of the scale, with the weight of the box displayed on the readout of your scale, so that your potential bidders on eBay can be confident in the accuracy of your auction. These potential bidders will be bidding based almost entirely on the weight of the scrap metal in the box, so they will want to be able to verify the exact weight of the product.

Next, dump out the box on a flat surface and take some photographs of the contents. If you have ornamental items in your box, take additional photos of those items. Download the photos to your computer, and then log in to your eBay account. Go to the 'Sell an Item' page on eBay. There are two categories that you can sell scrap metal in: Coins and Paper Money, Bullion and Business & Industrial, Metals & Alloys. List your scrap metal in one of these two categories.

Go to the photograph section and upload your digital photographs to your auction listing page. An example of a title I would use for my auction would be along the lines of: '24# (LBS) #1 SCRAP COPPER Bowls Pipes Decorations'. #1 Copper is the designation scrap dealers use for solid copper items, or large stripped copper wires with no insulation, and is the highest grade of copper. The additional descriptors may also get collectors of ornamental copper items to bid on your auction.

Make sure that you are accurate in your description of the auction. Subtract the weight of the box when providing the weight (usually about 8 ounces for a Large Flat Rate box). Under the Shipping section of the listing, click on 'Large Flat Rate Box', and use the 'Calculated Shipping' option, with an additional 1-2 dollars added, so that some of your eBay and PayPal fees are covered by the shipping cost.

List your auction. I like to start my auctions between 3:00 and 9:00 PM, as that as when the most users are on eBay.

When the auction is complete, seal the Flat Rate Box, address it with the winning bidder's address, and take it to the post office to ship it, or if you are already an internet seller, use your online shipping service and ship from home. It is as easy as that!

TO KEEP ASSEMBLED, OR DISASSEMBLE; THAT IS THE QUESTION!

One of the more difficult decisions in maximizing profits on large pieces of vintage electronics or machinery is figuring out whether to sell the entire item on EBay, or to take the item apart and sell the interior components.

There are several things that will affect your decision. The first is the overall size of the item. It is common to find large appliances, console stereos, exercise equipment and other similar-sized items with a 'FREE' sign on them along the roadways in any small town. Should you pick them up? Heck yes, you should.

The question then becomes, how do I sell this bulky piece of junk? Obviously, nobody is going to pay the shipping fees for shipping these items weighing several hundred pounds, unless the item is extremely valuable.

It is possible that you can sell the item on EBay, with a free local pickup option for the shipping method. The winning bidder then has to make arrangements with you to pick up the item after the auction is completed. You can also list the item on Craig's List or in the local classified section of your newspaper.

Selling the item whole is often the fastest and least time-intensive method of selling large items. There is almost zero preparation time, and you can often unload items in one week or less. You should sell items whole if you determine that the item is collectible in the condition you find it in (no restoration costs to you), and if you think somebody near you would want to buy it. This is often the case with audio equipment, juke boxes, large advertising items, and arcade games. These types of items have many collectors, and they will buy whole items whether they work, or not.

There are some issues to consider when selling whole items, such as the ones that we have discussed. The most important issue is that in order for you to sell the item, you have to know whether it works, or not. If you advertise that the item works, it had better be completely functional. This is especially true if you sell your item on EBay, as you do not want to receive negative feedback from your buyers, or nobody will want to bid on your auctions.

You may decide to advertise the item in 'As-Is' condition, which means that buyer or bidder is buying your item as they see it in the ad or auction page. 'As-Is' condition means that you are unsure of the operating condition of the machinery and components, or that you know that the machine does not work. This is often a safer way of selling large pieces of machinery with many moving parts.

You also have to keep in mind that old machinery that has not been used for a long period of time will often break down quickly when it is put back into use. In other words, if you test something for a couple of minutes and it seems to work fine, it may still break very soon after your buyer starts using the item. Then, you have to deal with possibility of having the buyer leave you negative feedback or having to at least partially refund the sales price because the item broke. Imagine how you would feel if you bought a cool collectible vintage juke box, and then it broke down after you played less than ten songs on it. You'd want your money back, right?

I honestly have sold very few large whole items, due to the problems I've already discussed. Nobody wants to pay shipping costs on these types of items, and gas prices prevent people from driving long distances to pick them up. It's also routinely more profitable to disassemble large items and sell the components on EBay.

I can remember multiple occasions, where I attempted to sell electronic items that weighed between ten and seventy pounds on EBay and received no bids at under $10, due to the shipping costs. After I received no bids, I disassembled the electronics and sold the components for 5 to 10 times that amount within several weeks.

One good example of this was a vintage 1960s console stereo / record player that we found at a garage sale for $5. We hauled it home and put in our basement. It worked great! It had a sharp looking wooden cabinet, and contained a radio, a record turntable, and even an 8- track player with some old working Elvis, Aerosmith and Johnny Cash tapes. I don't remember the manufacturer, but it was a mid-range brand name that I was familiar with. In other words, it was not a top-of-the-line collectible brand.

Everything worked great on the console, and I used it a lot when we first got it, and then less and less frequently over time. Eventually, we decided that the console took up a lot of room and we wanted to go another route with décor in the basement, so we tried to sell the stereo.

We listed the whole console on EBay for $20, with a free local pickup shipping method. It did not receive a bid for three re-lists at $20.

My wife wanted to put the console out for free at the roadside, but I said no. Even though this was at the beginning of our selling careers, I knew enough to take apart the console and try to sell the interior parts.

It has been about seven years since we sold the console, but from my recollection, it took about four hours to completely take it apart. It took a couple of hours to research which parts to sell on EBay, and another couple of hours to list the items. After about two weeks, I had sold the 8-track tapes for $20, the 8-track player for about $25, some parts off of the turntable for $15, two sets of large interior speakers for $35, the cloth wiring for $10, the tuner assembly for $15, and then scrapped the rest for another $20-30 in scrap copper and other metals. If I knew then what I know now, I would have made another $20-30 in selling name plates, the turntable stylus, the cloth speaker coverings, and other items, and also an extra $10+ in scrap gold and silver contacts. You get the point.

Recently, I helped my mother remove a 10-year old treadmill exercise machine from her house. I took it apart in less than an hour, and sold the motor for $25, the digital display for $15, the rollers for $10, the track for $5, and it had about $25 worth of scrap metal in it afterwards.

I found an old dead Pioneer tuner stereo at a garage sale for free about three years ago, and sold the oak case for $50, the metal screw-on feet for almost $20, and the name plate for another $10. I sold assorted components for another $20, and there was about $10 worth of scrap metal inside, mostly copper, aluminum and brass.

These are not just isolated incidents, I find this stuff all of the time.

If you think about it, the selling of components makes much more sense on many levels. The shipping cost for these smaller components is usually going to be under $10. People can afford to pay for shipping for parts, rather than paying significantly higher shipping costs for whole units.

There are many, many collectors of these types of vintage electronics. If you can think of a popular type of electronics, somebody probably collects them. Collectors enjoy tinkering with interior components, upgrading parts, and customizing their units. Plus, these old systems often break down, and parts fail. In other words, people that like these old machines need parts often, and these are the type of people who enjoy being on a computer and buying things online.

Vintage components are also very difficult to find at physical stores, even in metropolitan areas. Do remember seeing stores that sell vintage audio or computer components? Me either. It's much easier to go to EBay and find what you are looking for there, than to locate a physical store that sells vintage replacement parts.

MAXIMIZE PROFITS IN VINTAGE ELECTRONICS

There are several things that you will want to research BEFORE you take apart any vintage electronic item. As we discussed before, research Completed Items on EBay, and determine which components are worth selling. Again, you should know ahead of time which assemblies are better sold whole, and which assemblies should be broken down into even smaller components, or individual parts.

I have also provided you with an excellent free link, which describes in detail how to disassemble many different large electronics and appliances for scrap value.

Once you have an idea of which parts you will be removing for sale, take your item to a location where you can make a mess, but not lose any small parts. A large table top or countertop works well.

Gather you tools. The tools you will use most often are: both types of screwdrivers, needle-nose pliers, wire cutters, an adjustable wrench, a hammer (Oh, yeah! Breaking' stuff is fun!), a magnet, several large vinyl trash bag, and safety glasses.

You can greatly expedite the process with a cordless drill or power screwdriver with both driver bits. A power rotary tool (Dremel) with a supply of cut-off disks and a drill bit is well worth the investment, if you do not have one. I use mine constantly.

You may also need a set of sockets, and you will occasionally find exotic screw heads like star bits and Allen wrench heads, but if you have a rotary tool, you can cut off the screws, or make them into standard screwdriver heads by slicing them with the cut-off disk. You will also use the rotary tool often for cutting off rusted or stripped screws and bolts. It also cuts through thick copper cord insulation like butter, saving you tons of time!

Please heed a word of caution. Before you start breaking stuff, make sure you know what you are doing. Remember, in the 1950s and 60s, nobody even knew what a 'health code violation' was. Old electronics and appliances can contain some nasty stuff. There is mercury inside some old glass switches and components, for instance. You should not open anything that is sealed in glass, or welded shut, unless you know for sure what is inside.

OK, now that we got that out of the way, let's break some stuff. Start on the outside and CAREFULLY remove any decorative items, advertising badges, knobs, feet, etc., that you can sell. Remember, the plastic is going to be old and brittle on vintage items. If you snap the emblem in half, it is worthless. Believe me, I have broken some, even though I was being very careful. Even the glass in the display covers is more brittle in many older components.

After the outer pieces are removed, check EBay Completed Listings to see if the outer shell of your item can be sold. Often, the shells and cases of audio components, and even rotary telephones can be sold.

I usually start by using the cordless drill and unscrewing all of the screws that I can see on the outside of the device. Remove the outer shell, or the access panel to get at the interior of the item. If the shell is going to be sold, put it in your 'Sell' pile. If it is not going to be sold and it is plastic, throw it in your trash bag. If it is metal, hit it with a magnet. If it is ferrous, throw it in your 'Steel' pile. Sometimes the shell will be aluminum and should be saved in its own pile with other aluminum.

I save all of my screws, bolts and other connectors, as well. I put them all in a large coffee can. When it's full, I intend to sell the lot on EBay in the vintage electronics category for about $20. I also sometimes use various screws when I need them for household repairs, or sometimes screws are sold with components, and I need to replace a couple that I lost. Occasionally, you will find screws and bolts made of solid brass or aluminum. Save these in their respective scrap pile.

Now that you are into the interior of the item, find the components that you are looking to sell, and remove them. Put them in your Sell pile. Save the screws and attachments that affix the items that you are going to sell if possible and sell them with the component. If you lose a screw, do not worry about it. The screws are just insurance, in case the buyer needs them. They are not required.

Try to avoid clipping wires connected to components that you plan to sell. Carefully pull wires that have jacks or plugs from their ports using needle-nose pliers. Remember, your buyer is going to be hooking the component into his system, and is not going to want to splice wires, if it is avoidable. If there are multiple components available to buy on EBay, and some of the listings have the entire wires, with the plugs, and yours have clipped ends, your item will not get many bids, or will not sell if it is a fixed price auction.

Once all of your sellable components have been removed, the fun starts. Take one last look, and see if there might be anything else that you could sell that you did not find on EBay before. When you are satisfied that everything that could be sold has been removed, you are ready to start scrapping.

You should realize that there are also whole components that can be sold as scrap, on EBay, via an E-Scrap website, or at your local scrap yard. Internet sites such as Boardsort.com offer fixed prices for items such as computer hard drives, circuit boards, cellular telephones, and computer power supply boxes. You should check these sites so that you know what you will be saving, and the prices that are offered. Several of these sites are listed in the appendices of this document, with hyperlinks to their websites.

Now that you know what you are looking for, get out your USPS Priority Mail Flat Rate Boxes. Label the boxes with the materials that you intend to place in them. In addition, you will need extra-large boxes or totes for ferrous steel, and medium and low class circuit boards. You will have a lot of these materials.

I normally collect a fair amount of vintage electronics and appliance parts before I have a disassembly session, so that I can get a lot of scrap to sell at one time.

When I start scrapping, I always have the following Large Flat Rate boxes ready for material collection: Bare Copper, Insulated Copper, Bare Brass (It is OK to have copper attached to brass, and most scrap yards allow chrome covering over brass, as well), old aluminum, shiny aluminum (often aluminum heat sinks), and a smaller box for silver and gold contacts and components I intend to break down for precious metal content.

If there are computer hard drives in the pile, they usually require their own special boxes for material that will be sold separately, or sent to Boardsort.

I usually keep another box of copper / aluminum heat sinks, and later take the Dremel to the copper wire. If you use the cut-off disk on the Dremel, you can slice the copper all the way down to the spool, and then peel off the copper. Place the copper in your shiny copper box, and save the heat sink bases. They are often stainless steel, and can be sold separately at scrap yards for decent money. You will find a lot of large heat sinks in old electronics and appliances. I found a heat sink several days ago in a 1950s industrial washing machine that had almost ten pounds of copper spooled inside it. The stainless base weighed 18 pounds.

I also save all of my plug ends from electrical cords in a box, and later peel the prongs off with pliers or cut open the plug end with the rotary tool, and then remove the metal. Older plugs have brass prongs, and most newer plugs are made of shiny aluminum. You are required to cut the plug ends off of copper electrical cords before you can sell them at the scrap dealer, so you will be cutting off the plug ends, anyway.

Boardsort also offers a fixed rate for wire and cord connectors that contain gold. Many of the   computer connectors that resemble bristles at the ends or have many tiny holes, contain small amounts of gold and silver. Ribbon ends also frequently contain precious metals. You may decide to save these connectors in a box, and sell them on EBay, as well.

Most scrap dealers also buy components containing copper as 'Copper Breakage' or 'Electric Motors'. Save components containing copper in a box. Many of these components can also be easily broken open with a hammer or cut open with a Dremel, and then you can remove the copper and brass pieces that are inside to maximize your profits.

Make sure that you are keeping an eye out for precious metal contacts while you are scrapping. Old electronics and appliances can have relatively large contacts that are often pure silver, and sometimes gold. Look on the ends of brass and copper fingers where wires are connected, inside all electric motors, and inside any components that spin at high speeds or generate a lot of heat. Contacts can range in size from the width of a pencil lead all the way up to the diameter of a large watch battery.

Many gold contacts will be bright and shiny gold-colored buttons. They are easy to spot, as gold does not tarnish. Silver contacts can be more difficult to find, as they are often dulled and tarnished with age, and can blend in with the base material.

If you are unsure if the contacts are silver or gold, lightly scrape them with a screwdriver, or hit them with the Dremel disk. The will be bright and shiny under the exterior coating of grime. If you're still not sure, test with your gold tester, or throw them in your 'Gold and Silver' box and refine it with the rest of your material in the box later.

When you find good contacts, clip the button of silver or gold off, and then keep the base material for brass or copper scrap. Don't waste the whole brass or copper finger by refining it in your gold and silver material.

When you fill up the Flat Rate boxes, photograph the materials inside, weigh the box (take a photo of the box with the scale read-out), label the box with the weight, and then list the material on EBay, or save it to take to the scrap dealer.

The last step is the most important. Make sure that you clean up your mess after you are done bashing electronics! If you do your business inside, your significant other will not be happy with the end result of your destruction. If they are not happy, then you will not be happy either, right? If you have an outdoor shop or disassembly area, you should still clean up the mess. Metal pieces can be sharp, and kids or pets can get cut on them.

TREATING YOUR BUSINESS AS A BUSINESS: INCOME TAX ISSUES

You don't have to be an accountant or a business major in college to effectively manage your small business. In my opinion, the one thing that keeps the majority of internet sellers from graduating from a small-time operation into a real business is the failure to understand where they are making money and where they are losing profits.

On the surface this sounds like it would be common sense, but often, the sources of the issues are not as evident as you would think.

Anybody can look at their checking accounts and see how much money eBay or Amazon is depositing into them. But is that the bottom line profits of your business? Of course not.

I highly recommend keeping track of your profits and expenses on a spreadsheet, so that you can get a picture of your overall money flow.   There are many different spreadsheets online that you can tailor to your selling situation. Find one that you like and start using it from the outset of your selling or scrapping career. You will be very glad that you did.

Keeping your spreadsheet helps you in a number of different ways. First, you can see which segments of your selling are making you the most money. Second, you can find areas where you can save yourself money in over-expenditure on packaging supplies, storage fees, gas money, etc.

To illustrate the second point, I remember reviewing our numbers after one season of garage sailing. We thought that we were doing really well, because we were making good profits on a very high percentage of the items that we bought. However, after crunching numbers, we were not as happy. We were losing a lot of our profits in gas costs and meals while driving from sale to sale. Also, a lot of the items were we selling were large, bulky items, and were costing us more money for packaging supplies. We also realized that we were spending a lot of time and money driving to the post office with packages.

These discoveries that we made directly led to us changing where we bought inventory, how we kept track of travel expenses, and investing in using an internet postage and pick-up service.

Keeping track of your expenses also prepares you for completing your income taxes. Not only are you required to claim your income from internet sales on your income tax returns, your internet sales business can actually help you with your tax burden, or increase your refund.

This is especially true in the first year of your business, as you are allowed to claim start-up expenses for expenditures, such as computers, smart phones, Wi-Fi and high speed internet installation, storage units, shelving, desks and furniture, and other odds and ends that you need to start your business. Just ensure that you are using the items that you are going to claim as business expenses only for your business. If you use any of the items for personal use in any manner, you will need to adjust for this personal use. Failure to do so, could lead to large fines if you are audited.

Keeping you receipts organized is also very important. Not only does that allow you to see where you are spending your money, it is also necessary to be able to verify spending to claim them on your income tax returns. You can claim meals and other expenses while you are conducting your business (finding inventory), overhead costs (packaging tape, computer paper, etc.), and advertising expenses, but only if you have receipts to verify your claims.

Another very nice tax deduction you can claim is for your home office. If you have a portion of your home or other building that is used

EXCLUSIVELY for the execution of your business, you can claim that portion of your home's utilities, repairs, and property taxes on your income taxes. That can be a huge break. You can also claim the cost of the degradation to your office space and the furniture and appliances that you use in your business. All of the forms needed to claim these items are found on tax preparation applications, such as TurboTax. You may have to do some research, or ask you tax professional, but the time will be well spent.

Just make sure that you understand that if you claim a home business deduction, you will be more likely to be audited at some point. Ensure that you have reviewed the applicable IRS rules, and have receipts and paperwork to verify your deductions.

DONATIONS

Another way that you can save money is to donate items to Goodwill or similar non- profit organizations. This would include both your own personal items and your business inventory items that did not sell at auction or on Amazon.

One website that will greatly assist you in this area is www.ItsDeductible.com.   The website provides you an acceptable allowance to claim for a wide array of household items in two condition categories. For instance, a used vinyl record in average condition may be claimed for $2. The values are accepted by the IRS. You may be surprised how much a large box of clothing will allow you claim on you taxes. You can also claim the mileage for you to get from your home to the donation site.

You do not get to claim 100% of the value of the donations to Goodwill, but the amount that you can claim can be significant, if you donate continually throughout the year.

Make sure that you take pictures of the contents of the boxes and bags that you donate, and save them in a folder on your computer, so that you can verify what you have donated.

ItsDeductible is also partnered with TurboTax, and other tax prep applications. This allows the tax applications to directly download your information from your donations and mileage on your ItsDeductible page, and place the values in the correct areas of your return.

This is a huge time saver!

The proceeds from this document are dedicated to our children's college funds. I greatly appreciate your interest in my product. Please recommend this book to your friends and family. If you have a couple of minutes, please take the time to leave feedback on Amazon for this document by going to your account, and leaving a feedback / review for the order. Good luck in your future endeavors, Eric Michael.

A printable DVD version of this document is available on Amazon.

Like us on Facebook and talk about treasure hunting at http://www.facebook.com/almostfreemoney.

If you have questions please contact me at the following email address. My second book in the Almost Free Money is titled "Garage Sale Superstar", and focuses entirely on finding treasure at garage sales, yard sales and estate sales. Superstar is available on Kindle and in print on Amazon.

WEBSITES AND LINKS

Here are some very helpful websites and web pages to jump start your research. These are my favorites, after completing many hours of surfing (You are welcome!)

1. Garage Sale Academy

My website has a ton of information about how to become a garage sale picker, and how to resell your garage sale finds on the internet. It expands the information from Almost Free Money by adding an entire niche on garage sale picking / shopping, and tons of information on how to get the best deals at sale, and find the best swag. It also has another niche for increasing the productivity of garage sales, yard sales, and estate sales for sale hosts.

2. http://www.scrapmetaljunkie.com/scrap-metal-handbook-guide

I still can't believe this site is free. A tremendous amount of information, and well organized. The site provides a nice explanation on how to sort and identify scrap metals. This is the only site that I have found that provides step-by-step instructions on how to disassemble appliances and other large items for maximizing scrap recovery. Includes: How to take apart a TV, Computer, Washing Machine, Microwave, and many more items. Also has an excellent blog, with information from many experienced scrappers. Regardless of whether you are a beginner, or an experienced scrapper, if you have not been to this site, you will make money by spending time here.

3. http://www.scribd.com/doc/20327561/Scrap-Parts-Comp-Identific
    ation#outer_page_1

Scraper's Master Parts List: A nice summation of where you can find valuable
gold, silver and platinum in computers and other electronics. Indexed, with
photo identification of components like diodes, transformers, and capacitors
and where to find them within the electronics.

4. http://boardsort.com

This company will pay you up front through PayPal immediately upon
confirmation of your information with digital photo of your material. They pay
competitive prices for computer scrap, gold board fingers, and some other
related e-scrap. You have to pay for shipping, but they pay up front, which is
nice. They also have an updated price list of what they pay for a variety of
materials, so you know what you can expect to be paid when you send them
your scrap.

5. http://voices.yahoo.com/find-almost-free-gold-thrift-shops-yard-sal
    es-beginner-113530.html?cat=51

Also has a link for finding silver. Good explanation of the different
classifications of gold and silver, their markings on jewelry, and how to find it
for cheap at garage sale, thrift shops, etc.

6. http://fairsalvage.com/material_info.html

A sample page from a scrap metal yard - good descriptions of different
classifications of scrap.

7. http://fairsalvage.com/pricing_clare.html

A sample price list from the same scrap yard.

8. http://www.ehow.com/how_7830442_refine-gold-plating.html

How to refine your scrap and plated gold to .995 pure. Requires chemicals and safety equipment. **Do this at your own risk.**

9. http://shorinternational.com/RefineAgInstruct.php

How to refine plated silver and silver contacts to .995 pure silver. Alternate method using household chemicals. **Do this at your own risk.**

10. http://cointrackers.com/is-my-coin-silver.php

Good information on silver coins, and actual silver content. Did you know that a 1963 US quarter is worth $2.09 due to silver content?!

11. https://www.auctiva.com

EBay listing web site. We use this exclusively for making our EBay listings. You get free templates and scrolling display, which lets visitors on your auctions see all of your other ongoing auctions.

12. https://itsdeductibleonline.intuit.com

As discussed in Donations section. Provides IRS-accepted values for your donations, and keeps track of your donations for the entire tax year. Inserts your donations into online Income Tax forms such as TurboTax.

13. http://used.addall.com

Free book search with values, used for finding values for rare and collectible books. Save this to your favorites, you should be using this site on a regular basis.

14. http://pulse.ebay.com

Provides a 'Hot List' for EBay completed listings.

15. http://www.isoldwhat.com

Has entire listing of EBay categories, and also number of individual listings for each category and subcategory. Also has Amazon browse counts by category.

16. http://www.metalprices.com

Spot prices for most precious and scrap metals, plus historical prices.

Appendices

TABLE 1: Usable Items, TABLE 2: Collectible Items

Item	Where	Description
Air Conditioners, Parts	20711	Scrap - Lots of copper in old ACs
Archery Equipment	20835	Bows, Arrows, Shafts, Tabs, Guards
Audio / Video, Vintage and Parts	175740	
Baby Food Containers [glass,	57736	Used for craft supply storage
Baby Food Containers, Plastic +	83893, 44912	Used for Beads, Fly-Making Supply Holders
Bar Items and Accessories	3265	Bar Sets, Corkscrews, Pitchers, Taps, etc
Bar Tools	20687	
Barn Doors and Hardware	162926	Vintage doors $300-800, Iron Hardware VG
Barn Wood	84011	Sold by board, or sell locally Craigs List
Baseball and Softball Gear	16021	
Batteries, Rechargeable	48619	Any batteries that work - Can be $40
Battery Compartment Covers	Ebay	List in category of complete unit
BBQ Grill Tools	20725	
Beach Glass (Surf Polished glass)	41221	
Beads from Vintage Costume	156281	Bakelite, colorful
Bells, Small to Medium	71110	Used for Hunting Dog Locators
Bike Accessories	22688	
Bike Parts, Newer Bikes	57262	
Bike Parts, Vintage	56197	Some worth quite a lot - Easier to part them
Billiards / Pool Balls	75192	
Billiards Accessories	75184	Cues, Balls, Racks, Decor
Bird Houses	20502	Home Made VG
Board Game Parts, Dice, Pieces	7317	Check out everything you can sell
Board Games and Parts	233, Amazon	here!
Book Dust Jackets, Illustrations	121833	Pick up any Sealed games for
Bottle Caps	160732	Scrapbooking, Crafts
Bottles, Wine	38172	For Wine Making
Bowling Ball Bags, Vintage	169291	Sell for $10-50 as Women's Purses
Bowling Gear	20846	
Boxes [Empty]	Ebay	Electronics Boxes can be worth $20!
Boxes [Empty] Small	83893, 44912,	Fly, Bead Storage, Also shipping
Brass Bullet Shells	57736	Jewelry
[Empty] Brass, Scrap	SMD, CL	For Reloading, Scrap Value
Building Toys Lots	29402, SMD	
Butter Containers w/Lids	18991	Esp. Legos -random lots
[Empty] Cabinet Hardware	Ebay	Lots of 20 -Various categories
Calls, Hunting	36252	Can be $50 - Sterilize and sell
Camping and Hiking Gear	16034	Vintage or Not

Candles	46782	Yankee Candle VG
Carbide Steel Scrap	29402, SMD	Drill Bits, tool ends,
Cases from Vintage Electronics	175741	Audio Receiver Cases
Cases, Plastic [Empty]	Ebay	Everybody wants these for storage
Caster Wheels, Vintage	162913	
Catalytic Converters,	29402, SMD	From autos, worth $20-150
Scrap CD Cases	307	
CD/DVD/Media Racks	22653	Easy to Find, Can be sold on Amazon
Chainsaw Parts	85915	Bars, Chains, Guards, Cases
Cigar Cases/Tubes [Empty]	156508	Cigar Display, also used for crafts supplies
Clothing, Vintage	91235, 91244	Old Ties, Suits, Dresses
Computer Board Gold Fingers	29402, SMD	Trim off w/wire cutters, shears
Computer Boxes	175690	Plus boxes for Accesories and
Computer CPUs Processors	164	Sold Single or lots, can be scrapped for gold
Computer Games, PC	175690	Floppy Disks, Cassettes, etc
Computer Motherboards	1244	Sold as replacements, or scrapped (- gold
Computer Parts, Vintage	175690	Apple 2e, Commodore, etc
Computer Power Supplies	42017	Replacement Parts, or scrap
Computer, Cards	175690	Sound Cards, Video Cards
Computer, Logos	175690	Emblems, etc -Old Apple, Commodore, etc
Computer, Manuals & Paperwork	175690	
Computer, Outer Cases	175690	
Computer, Software and Disks	175690	
Computers, Circuit Boards	175690	For Parts, Rebuilding Computers, or Scrap
Computers, Components	175690	Cords, Joysticks, Mice, Disk Drives, etc
Computers, IC Chips	175690	Scrap for Gold, or Collectible -Some Big $
Computers, Memory	175690	Scrap Value, additional Mem for PCs
Computers, Parts	175690	
Computers, Vintage	171957	Working or Not
Containers, Prescription Drug	83893, 44912, 57736	Used for Craft, Fly-Making Holders
Containers, Skin Care [Empty]	11862	Used for Making Travel Kits, Refills
Cookware	20628	Old Cast Iron items VG
Copper, Scrap	29402, SMD	
Cords, cables for Electronics	14961, SMD	
Corks, Wine	71177	For Crafts, Wine Making
Cornhole Toss Game Bags	79791	Easy to Make, Easy to Sell
Coupons	172010	
Coupons and Gift Cards	172008	
Croquet Items	117210	Vintage Balls $10, Wicket Sets $10,
Crosses, Decorative	75570	Altered Art, Collage, Steampunk Art
Darts, Dartboards	26328	
Decoys, Hunting	36249	If you see cheap decoys, buy them!
Decoys, Hunting Accessories	36249	Duck decoy anchors, hooks, lines
Dice	7317	Used for Crafts, Scrapbook, Jewelry

Item	Code	Notes
Dinnerware, Serving Pieces	36027	
Doll Parts	75570	Altered Art
Dominoes	2555	Collectible, or Mixed Lots used for Crafts
Door Hardware & Knobs	37911	Glass Knobs, Ornate Knobs VG
Door Hardware, Parts	41976	Knobs, Hinges, Locks, Handles, Locksets
DVD Cases [Empty]	617	
Eyeglass Frames	SMD	Vintage Frames were Gold-Filled
Fabric, Vintage	28162	Anything from old drapes, upholstery, etc
Fabrics, Vintage	38000	From Bolts, Furniture seats, Blankets, etc
Face Plates, Vintage Audio	175741	
Fasteners, Screws, Nails	20600	
Feet, Vintage Electronics	14998	Cushioned Feet from Audio best
Film Containers -Empty 35mm	4201	Lots of 10+ used for crafts, beads, flies
Fishing Accessories	72603	
Fishing Lures	31689, 36153	
Fishing Lures - Broken, Parts	165931	Especially from Vintage, Lips, Bodies
Fishing Lures, Empty Boxes	31689	
Fishing Pole Parts	62153	For Pole Repair, Building -Guides, Handles
Fishing Rod Guides, Handles	62153	Take from Broken Fishing Rods
Fishing Sinker Containers	83893, 44912	Used for Beads, Fly-Making Supply
Fishing, Fly	23810	High $ Items -Rods, Creels
Fishing, Freshwater	36145	
Fishing, Ice	36152	Can be worth more than regular fishing
Fishing, Saltwater	23821	
Flash Cards, Number Cards	75570	Altered Art, Collage
Flatware, Silverware	20693	Older are Silverplate, scrap value
Football Gear	21214	
Frames, Picture (Antique)	40024	
Furniture Parts, Pieces (Antique)	162913	Handles, Arms, Legs, Rails, Trim, etc
Garden Decor	20498	Chimes, Flags, Sun Dials, Water Items
Garden Supplies	2032	
Garden Tools	29515	
Gears and Cogs, Metal	75570	Altered Art, Steampunk
Gears, Sprockets	75570	For Altered Art, Collage Crafts
Glass, Polished and Smooth	163778	Beach polished better
Golf Balls	18924	Used lots, or vintage balls worth $
Golf Club Headcovers	18930	
Golf Clubs	115280	Singles, or Sets -Drivers VG

Item	Code	Notes
Greeting Cards [Vintage]	121833	For Scrapbooking
Grill, Gas Parts	20724	Knobs, wheels, grills, elements, burners
Guitar Parts	159953	Part out broken guitars for good money
Guitars	159953	Complete or Broken can still sell
Gun Parts	73943	Magazines, Choke Tubes, Barrels
Handles, Drawers & Cabinets	20601	Vintage, Glass, Brass
Handles, Plumbing Valves	37911, 75570	Cast Iron, Aluminum (Painted better)
Heaters, Furnace Parts	41987	
Horse Shoes, Tossing	79790	Singles or Sets
Hunting Accessories	52502	
Hunting Clothing	36239	Camouflage clothing -Army Surplus
Hunting Knives	42574	
Hunting Reloading Supplies	31823	
Hunting Taxidermy	36271	Worth VG $ - see quite often at sales
Jelly Jars [Empty]	28114	Canning, Making Candles, Storage
Jewelry Costume	500	
Jewelry for Parts and Repair	168176	Can get good money for broken jewelry!
Jewelry Pieces, Parts from Broken	164353	For Jewelry Making, Repair
Jewelry, Costume [Vintage]	500	
Jewelry, Loose Beads	488	Can sell beads from Old Furniture, Lamps
Kitchen Tools, Gadgets	20635	
Knobs, Furniture Handles	37911	Restorations, etc
Knobs, Vintage Electronics	14998	Especially from high-end Audio -Bakelite
Lamp Parts and Pieces	13865	Fillials, Knobs, Hanging Hardware
Lawn Mower Parts, Accessories	82248	Sell the Wheels, Seat, Blades then Scrap
Letter Tiles, Scrabble [Wooden]	19097	For Crafts, Scrapbooking, Lots of 100 best
Logos / Emblems	Ebay	From old Electronics, Cars, Bikes, etc
Luggage and Travel Bags	16085	
Magazines	280	Print Ads, Articles may be worth more
Make-up and Accessories	31786	Includes Vintage Make-up
Manuals / Instructions	Ebay	Sell in Vintage Electronics
Media, Blank (Vintage)	64627	Reel to Reel, Cassettes, All Kinds
Metal, Alloys, Scrap Metal	29402, SMD	
Microwave Parts	150138	Sell Glass Trays $20+, Magnitrons,
Motors, Electric	175741	Can sell small Motors as Lot
Motors, Electric Scrap	29402, SMD	Also copper windings and breakage
Music CDs, Vinyl Records, Tapes	11233	Sell as singles or in lots
Musical Instruments, Brass	16212	Usually parts worth more than Brass Scrap

Nail Polish and Accessories	11871	Sell in Lots
Nails, Square (Vintage)	162930	Crafts, Vintage Restorations
Number Tiles, Rummikub Game	7317	Used for crafts, scrapbooking
ORV Parts and Accessories	Ebay Motors	
Outdoor Holiday Decor	117416	
Outdoor Power Equipment & Parts	29518	Blowers, Edgers, Weed Whips, Hedgers
Oven / Range Parts	43566	Knobs, Motors, Elements, Handles, Burners!
Oven Burners / Elements	43566	
Oven Racks	43566	$20-40 for good condition
Paint Brushes, Vintage	28110	
Paper Dolls and Clothing	75570	Altered Art, Collage
Patio Furniture Parts, Pillows	20716	
Perfumes and Colognes, Vintage	26396	Can be worth more than you would think
Photographs, Vintage	14277	
Ping Pong Paddles	36277	
Plumbing and Parts	20601	Parts or Scrap
Plumbing Fixtures, Handles	167948	Antique Brass, Cast Iron, Ceramics
Pool Toys	159921	
Portable Audio, Headphones	15052	Even vintage Walkman
Posters and Prints	41511	
Pottery Pieces, Shards	18875	
Power Strips, Surge Protectors	67779	Or scrap copper
Push-Up Pop Containers	102391	Used for Making Cupcake Shooters, Jell-O
Railroad Ties	Local, CL	For Landscaping
Recipes	20475	
Reel to Reel Tapes, Spools	14998	VG
Refridgerator / Freezer Parts	71259	Handles, Racks $20-40, Drawers $20
Remote Controls, Electronic	Ebay	Old Remotes can be worth $25+
Shoe Boxes, Vintage [Empty]	163628	Old Nike Boxes have been sold for $75!
Shoes, Vintage	163628,	80s Tennis Shoes, Old Wing Tips Women
Shotgun Shell Boxes [Empty]	71116	Used for Reloading
Shotgun Shell Hulls [Empty]	Reloading	For Reloading and Christmas Lights!
Showerheads	71282	
Skateboard Parts	159073	
Skateboarding Clothing	159077	
Skateboards	16264	
Sleds and Tubes	59892	
Snow Plows and Parts	Ebay Motors	Hoses, Lights, Control Pieces Easily
Speakers, Vintage or Not	50597	Even emblems from Speakers worth $
Spikes, Railroad	95163	Used for Coat Hooks, Knife Handles
Spools, Empty 620 Film	167943	For Vintage Film reloading $7/Pc
Spools, Empty Thread (Wood)	14083	
Spools, Ribbon [Empty]	71224	
Spools, Wire [Empty]	100180	

Sporting Goods Equipment	382	
Sporting Goods, Used	159043	Almost anything has value if it works
Spray Dispensers [Empty]	1277	Used for Making Gift Baskets, Potpourri
Telephones and Parts	3286	Entire Phones, Batteries, Battery Doors
Tennis and Racquet Gear	159134	
Thermostats and Parts	115947	
Tools, Hand	3244	
Tools, Power	3247	
Tooth Brushes, Used		Use for Cleaning Collectibles, Gun Cleaning
Toy Parts	1198	Vintage Tonka, Metal Parts, Part out old
Toys, Broken and Parts, Vintage	1198	Pieces & Parts of old toys, cars
Tractor, Agricultural Parts	160934	
Transformers, Power	175741	
Traps, Animal	71108	Good $$
T-Shirts, Vintage	28022	Rock Concert Shirts, Character, TV Shows
Tubes, Cosmetics [Empty]	88433	Lotion Tubes, etc -Clean, $7 for 20
Tubes, Plastic	159046	Lidded, Used for Geocaches
Tubing, Aluminum, Copper, etc	29402, SMD	
Tupperware Containers	20625	Especially pre-1980s
Turntables for Records, and	48649	
Turtle Shells	71129	
Typewriter Keys	75570	Old Flat Keys Best -Altered Art, Steampunk
Vacuum Parts, Vintage	42146	
Vehicle Air Cleaner Assemblies	Ebay Motors	
Vehicle Body Parts	Ebay Motors	Can be worth a lot of $
Vehicle Buttons, Controls	Ebay Motors	From Radios, Heaters, Dials, Displays
Vehicle Catalytic Converters	Ebay or SMD	$20-120 at scrap metal dealer
Vehicle Cup Holders, Storage	Ebay Motors	
Vehicle Floor Mats	Ebay Motors	
Vehicle Gas Caps	Ebay Motors	
Vehicle Gauges, Displays	Ebay Motors	Can be VG from old cars
Vehicle Glove Box Doors	Ebay Motors	
Vehicle Headlights and Rings	Ebay Motors	Easily removable and sold
Vehicle Hub Caps, Rims	Ebay Motors	
Vehicle Instrument Panels	Ebay Motors	
Vehicle Interior Panels	Ebay Motors	
Vehicle Interior Upholstery	Ebay Motors	
Vehicle Light Bulbs, Ext & Int	Ebay Motors	Can be good $ from working vintage lights
Vehicle Lighters	Ebay Motors	Easily Lost and Sold
Vehicle Logos, Hood Ornaments	Ebay Motors	Collectible!
Vehicle Mirrors	Ebay Motors	Easily Broken and sold
Vehicle Motor Parts	Ebay Motors	scrap the copper wires
Vehicle Parts, Vintage	Ebay Motors	Any salvagable parts
Vehicle Pedals and Pads	Ebay Motors	
Vehicle Seat Belts	Ebay Motors	Easily sold
Vehicle Spark Plug Wires	Ebay Motors	Easily removed and sold
Vehicle Tire Caps	Ebay Motors	These can be sold off old tires
Vehicle Towing Accessories	Ebay Motors	Hitches, Balls, Wiring Harnesses
Vehicle Trim, Chrome, Vintage	Ebay Motors	

Item	Code	Notes
Turn Signals & Light Covers	eBay Motors	
Vehicle Visors	eBay Motors	Easily removed &sold
Vehicle Wheel Lug Nuts	eBay Motors	Sets are better
Vehicle Wiper Assemblies	eBay Motors	
Vehicle, Door / Window Handles	eBay Motors	
Vials, Centrifuge / Lab (plastic)	159046	Geocaches 10/$8
Video Game Cases [Empty]	1249	Newer Consoles
Video Game System Parts,	54968	For any console
Video Games	1249	
Wall Decor	38233	
Wall Decor, Metal Art	38233	
Wallpaper	42135	Even Vintage Rolls
Washers and Dryers Parts	71256	Handles, Belts, Motors
Washers, 2.5"	79790	Washer Toss Game
Watch Faces	160645	Beading, Altered Art
Watch, Clock Hands	75570	Altered Art
Watches and Parts	14324	
Wedding Items	11827	
Weed Whip Parts	71278	Guards, heads
Window Parts	63514	Finials, Tie-Backs
Windows, Screens, Parts	20592	
Wine Charms	31591	Easy to make, Sell well
Wine Glass Holders	159901	
Winter Sports Gear	36259	Skiing, Snowshoe
Wiring, Cloth-Covered Copper	175741	For Vintage Electronics
Yarn	36589	Especially vintage
1950s Items	69853	
1960s Items	69854	Retro, Lucite, Bakelite
1970s Items	69855	
Advertising Collectibles	34	Colas, John Deere,
Advertising Items	34	Pick Up any Free Items
Aprons	13951	
Archery, Vintage Items	158960	Broadheads, Wood arrows
Ash Trays	594	
Autographs and Signed Items	14429	
Automobilia, Collectibles	14024	License Plates, Spark Plugs, Advertising
Aviation items	14049	
Bakelite Plastic Items	72397	If you don't know what Bakelite is, find out!
Banks	66503	

Beads, Vintage	156281	Bakelite, Retro, Ceramics best
Bears, Teddy	386	
Beer Collectibles	562	Advertising, Signs, Tins, Cans, Bottle Caps
Bikes, Vintage Frames Parts	159000	Frames, Handle Bars, Forks, Guards,
Billiards Balls	75192	
Boat and Ship items	14052	
Bottle Caps	158421	Look for Cork lined caps
Bottles	39491	
Bottles, Antique	29797	Early Coke, Pepsi worth hundreds
Bowling, Vintage Items	159100	
Building Toys	18998	Legos, Tinker Toys, Lincoln Logs
Buttons	41195	Look for Military, Character Buttons
Calculators, Vintage	58042	
Calendars	41183	
Calls, Duck Hunting	36252	Plus Goose, Turkey -good $
Candle Holders	4062	
Cards, Greeting (vintage)	35889	Also sold for collages, crafts
Cards, Playing	1438	Can be sold as decks, or singles (Pairs)
Cartoons and Characters	1344	
Casino Collectibles	898	Chips, Dice, Advertising, Apparel
Cast Iron Items	3631	Table and Kitchen Items, Wall Decor, Toys
China, Dinnerware	24	Sets $$
Christian Items	11668	
Christmas Collectibles	13877	Very Abundant and Worth Good Money
Christmas Decorations	907	Ornaments, Decor, Nativities
Clocks	397	Even 1970s Alarm Clocks, Bakelite
Coasters	13907	
Coasters	13907	Sets much better
Corals	165715	
Costume Jewelry, Beads	156281	
Crucifixes and Crosses	11669	
Decorative Collectibles	13777	Plates, Figurines, Curios, Baskets
Decoys, Hunting	71131	Early Duck decoys worth hundreds
Disney Items and Characters	137	Can be worth a lot of $
Drapes, Curtains	942	Vintage, retro Fabric
Dreidels	165694	
Fabric, Vintage	29817	Lengths of Vintage Fabric can be up to
Fantasy, Magic Items	10860	Unicorns, Skulls, Gargoyles, Dragons
Fast Food Toys	19077	
Fishing Decoys, Spearing	793	Old carved decoys over $100
Fishing Items, Vintage	792	Fly Rods & Reels worth hundreds
Fishing Lures, Vintage	36169	Can be worth a lot of $$
Fishing Reels, Vintage	36175	Complete or Parts - Easy to find, worth good
Fishing Rods	11144	Vintage or not
Fishing Tackle Boxes	793	
Fishing Taxidermy	159028	Finished Mounts can be over $100, $50 for
Fishing, Fly	23810	
Fishing, Vintage Items	792	
Flags and Pennants	13881	
Flashlights	13863	

Flies, Fishing	11142	
Football, Vintage Items	159120	
Fraternal Organizations	402	Scouts, Lions Club, Kiwanis, Knights
Frisbees	19017	
Games, Handheld Electronic	19072	Easy to find, older ones worth good $
Glass, 40s-60s	4207	Anchor-Hocking, US, Fenton
Glass, Art	955	
Glass, Carnival	2668	Fenton, IN Glass Cos.
Glass, Crackle	2712	
Glass, Depression	1002	Anchor Hocking, IN, US Glass
Glass, Pyrex	4765	
Glass, Vaseline	4935	Bright Yellow-Green Glass
Golf Balls, Vintage	18924	
Golf Club Headcovers	18930	
Golf Items, Vintage	83041	Balls, Bag Tags, Score Cards, Ads, Clothes
Greeting Cards, Vintage	35889	
Gun Parts, Vintage	71131	
Halloween Collectibles	14285	Can be worth more than you think
Halloween Items	907	Actually worth more than Christmas items!
Historical Items	13877	Police, Fire Depts, Orgs,
Holiday Decorations	907	
Horse Shoes, Tossing Vintage	79790	For Horseshoes game - Can be $20 set
Hunting, Vintage Items	71131	
Insulators, Glass & Ceramic	795	Can be found near existing power lines
Jars, Cookie	4047	Character Jars VG
Jewelry, Vintage and Antique	48579	Brooches, too!
Jewish Items	13773	
Key Chains	38016	
Kitchen Items	81	Utensils, Cannisters, Table Ware,
Kites	2569	
Knives	1401	Old Swiss Army Knives!
Lace and Doilies, Vintage	945	
Lamps, Electric	4053	
Lamps, Oil	4057	
Legos		Even newer Lego Sets, Men can be $30
Letters, Correspondences	156488	Love Letters, Military Letters
Lighters	951	Vintage Lighters can be worth $200+
Lunch Boxes and Thermoses	1409	Do not have to be Character boxes!
Magnets	476	
Maps and Atlases	37958	Can be worth good $
Maps, Vintage	1412	
Marbles	771	Can be big $ for old marbles
Maritime Antiques	37965	Bells, Anchors, Nets, Ship Items
Match Books	156496	
Medical, Dental Items	4065	
Menorrahs	13775	
Menus, Restaurant	1437	
Militaria	13956	Especially Civil War and WW2 items
Models, Vintage	1188	Unassembled worth much more
Motorcycle Items	10958	
Mugs, Coffee	38148	
Music CDs, Records, Tapes	11233	Records and obscure CDs best

Napkins, Vintage	165662	Packs Old Halloween Napkins $30-50
Night Lights	157010	
Other Holiday Collectibles	907	St Patricks, Valentines, etc
Pewter Items	1434	
Pez Dispensers	4097	Look for items with no feet
Photographs, Vintage	14277	
Pin Cushions	1465	
Pins (Pinbacks)	50787	Look for Obscure Campaign Buttons
Plastic Retro Items	108962	Lucite, LustroWare, Serving Pieces
Police Collectibles	928	Old Badges worth big $
Political Items	4100	Campaign Pins, Posters
Post Cards	914	
Pottery, Art	27	Can be worth a lot of $$
Print Advertisements	34	or Sell in Subject Matter Category
Puzzles, Jigsaw	2613	Wood, Springbok Circular Puzzles VG
Quilts	947	
Radios, Vintage + Parts	931	Part out broken radios!
Retro, Vintage Items	69851	BAKELITE, Hippie, Mod Art pieces
Science Fiction and Horror	152	Star Wars, Trek, X-Files, UFOs, Aliens
Sewing Items, Vintage	113	
Shakers, Salt and Pepper	4049	Characters, Should be Pair
Shells	82515	Sea Shells, Conches, Sand Dollars
Shot Glasses	3273	
Signs, Antique	63519	Ceramic, 2-Sided best
Silverplate Items	1436	
Skateboarding Items	16262	
Skateboards	16264	
Skateboards, Vintage & Parts	114248	
Slot Cars	2616	
Souvenirs and Travel	165800	By State, Country -Spoons, Patches, Mugs
Spools, Thread (Sewing)	14083	Look for old wooden spools
Sports Cards	212	
Sports Memorabilia	50123	
Stamps	260	Can be attached to Envelopes
Swizzle Sticks, Vintage	10905	Bakelite, Metal Handles
Table Linens, Cloths	13954	
Tarot Cards	35837	
Telephones, Vintage + Parts	38036	Parts often worth more than the entire
Thermometers, Barometers	14020	
Thimbles	38060	
Tin Items	10950	Collectible Tin Containers
Tobacco Items	593	
Toleware Items, Decor	1218	Antique Painted, Floral
Tools	4121	Especially Planes, Old Saws, Farm Items

Tools, Vintage	4121	Esp. Skeleton Keys, Planes, Forged Tools
Toy Soldiers	2631	Don't have to be that old
Toys, Action Figures	246	
Toys, Antique	717	
Toys, Building	18991	Legos worth $, Tinker Toys, Lincoln Logs
Toys, Celluloid	722	From 40s, 50s - $20-100
Toys, Die Cast Vehicles	222	Matchbox, Hot Wheels cars, examples
Toys, Tin	735	
Toys, Wind-up	74986	
Train and Railroad Items	1444	
Traps, Animal (Metal)	71131	Some old traps worth over $1000
Trivets	11656	
Trucking and Semi Items	35976	
Tubes (from Inside Electronics	64627	Can be worth $50 matched pairs, quads
Tupperware	13934	
TV, Movie, Character Toys	2624	Look for popular 80s TV shows, movies
Vanity Collectibles	597	Hair Items, Shaving, Perfumes
Vintage Bicycles and Parts	35959	
Watches	14324	
Waterford Crystal / Glass	7291	
Weather Vanes and Balls	37918	Antique Iron -Worth $100s
Wicca and Pagan Items	35831	
Yo-Yos	2664	Duncan, old wood

ORGANIC TTEMS

Driftwood	66789, 1285,	Aquariums, Terrariums, Taxidermy, Signs
Skulls, Animal	45604	
Bones, Animal	45604, 36271,	Taxidermy, Animal Collectors, More
Pine Cones	103479	Crafts, Wreath Making
Mushrooms, Morel	115722, Local	
Mushrooms,	115722, Local	
Nuts, Walnuts	25460	
Nuts, Pecans	25460	
Berries, [Wild]	25460	
Berries, Blackberries	25460	
Leeks [Wild Onions]	115722, Local	
Asparagus [Wild]	115722, Local	
Berries, Cranberries	25460	
Boughs, Pine & Cedar	Local	For Wreath Making, Holiday Crafts
Burls, Wood	3127	For Wood Carving, Turning. Can be $1000
Wood Blanks for	71235	Carving, Turning - Nice Grains
Antlers, Sheds	71124, 45604	
Eggs, Blown	116639	Empty Shells for Crafts -Ducks, Chicken,
Feathers, Bird	45220, 41199	HOT for Hair Accessories, Colorful
Feathers, Goose	41199	Domestic - For Blankets, Coats

Feathers, Duck	44913	Fly Tying
Fur, Rabbit, Hare	87096	Fly Tying
Deer Tails	87096	Fly Tying
Squirrel Tails	87096	Fly Tying, Lure Making
Fur, Other Animal	87096, 71130	Fly Tying - Woodchuck $3, Squirrel
Wood Plaques	71130	Background for Taxidermy- Cedar, Oak,
Hives, Bees Hornets,	71130	Taxidermy -MAKE SURE THEY'RE EMPTY
Coral	169311	Aquariums
Rocks, Stones for	66793	Holey Rocks up to $25 a piece
Stones, Beach/River	66793	Polished
Sea Shells	82515, 116418	Sea Shell Collectibles, Aquarium
Stone, Petoskey	3215	Up to $50 for Large -Polished or Rough
Stones, Pudding	3215	
Fossils	3215	
Agates	3215	
Petrified Wood		
Horns, Bull	71130	Taxidermy
Cottonwood Bark	160675	For Carving - $20/8 pcs
Basswood, Walnut	160675	Cut to blocks for carving
Star Fish	157019	
Sand Dollars	157016	
Sea Shells	82515	Large Conch Shells can be $20+
Meteorites, Tektites	3239	Meteorites can be worth $1000s

DEFINED VALUE ITEMS

ITEM	WHERE TO SELL	NOTES
Air Conditioner Compressors	SMD	$3
Alternators, Vehicle	SMD	Abt $4
Auto Bodies	SMD	$300+
Batteries, Lithium-Ion	SMD	At least .60 / LB
Calculators, Graphing	BuyBackWorld.com	$4-20
Cam Corders	Various Internet	
Cameras, Digital	Various Internet	
Cartridges, Ink Toner	Various Internet	
Catalytic Converters	Various Internet, SMD	
Cellular Telephones	Various Internet	Working Phones $80, Junk phones $4
Circuit Boards Gold Fingers	E-Scrap Sites	
Circuit Boards, Clean	E-Scrap Sites	
Circuit Boards, Populated	E-Scrap Sites	High =Gold Fingers, Low -VCRs, TVs
Computer Backplanes	E-Scrap Sites	
Computer Daughter	E-Scrap Sites	

Boards		
Computer Diodes	E-Scrap Sites	
Computer EPROMS	E-Scrap Sites	
Computer Hard Drive Boards	E-Scrap Sites	
Computer Hard Drives -Whole	E-Scrap Sites	
Computer IC Chips	E-Scrap Sites	
Computer Memory (RAM)	E-Scrap Sites	
Computer Mother Boards	E-Scrap Sites	
Computer Processors -PCUs	E-Scrap Sites	Ceramic, older CPUS can be collectible -Big $
Oxygen Sensors, Vehicle	Various Internet	Abt $3 / LB
Pager Boards	E-Scrap Sites	
Printer Cartridges, Empty	Various Internet	Values $1.25 - $20 (Have gold in heads)
Radiators, AL	SMD	$3
Radiators, Copper	SMD	$15, or $1.65 /LB
SIM, Smart Card Scrap	E-Scrap Sites	
Starters, Vehicle	SMD	Abt $4
Tantalum Resistors, Chips	TantalumRecyclers.com	
Telecom Boards	E-Scrap Sites	
Text Books	Various Internet	Usually better on Amazon
Transistors	E-Scrap Sites	
Transmissions, Vehicle	SMD	$10-35
Video Game Systems	Various Internet	
Wheels, Aluminum	SMD	$10 ea

Made in the USA
San Bernardino, CA
07 June 2014